FAMILY LETTERS

Parents and Children

My sonne that I see you not before my pairteing impute it to this great occasion quhairin tyme is sa precieuse, but that shall by goddis grace shortlie be recompenced by youre cum-ing to me & continuall residence with me euer after; lett not this newis maik you prowde or insolent for a kings sonne & heire was ye before, & na maire are ye yett, the augmentation that is heirby lyke to fall unto you, is but in cairis, & thou-raie burthens, be thairfor merrie but not insolent, keepe a greatnes but sine fastu, be resolute but not willfull, keepe youre kyndnes but in honorable sorte, choose nane to be youre playe fellowis but thaime that are well borne, & aboue all things giue neuer goode countenance to any but according as ye shall be informed that thay are in estimation with me, looke upon all englishe men that shall cum to visite you as upon youre louing subiectis, not with that ceremonie as touardis steraingeris, & yett with suche hairdines as at this tyme thay deserue, this gentleman quhom this beairare accumpanies is worthie & of guide rank, & now my familiare seruiteure, use him thairfore in a maire hamelie louing sorte nor otheris, I sende you heirwith my booke latelie prentid, studdie & profite in it as ye wolde deserue my blessing, & as thaire can na thing happen unto you quhairof ye will not finde the generall groundis thairin, if not the verrie particulaire pointe touched, sa man ye leuell euerie mannis opinions or aduyces unto you as ye finde thaime agree or discorde with the reulis thairin, sett doun, allowing & following thaire aduyces that agreeis with the same, mistrusting & frowning upon thaime that aduyses you to the contraire, be diligent & earnest in youre studdeis that at youre meiting with me I maye praise you for youre progresse in learning, be obedient to youre maister for youre awin weill & to procure my thankis, for in reuerencing him ye obeye me & honoures youre selfe. fairweill.

youre louing father.

James R

FAMILY LETTERS

Parents and Children

Edited by

JAN FIELDEN

First published in 1994 by
Marginalia Press,
an imprint of
Ippon Books Ltd
55 Long Lane,
London N3 2HY

ISBN (Hardback): 1 874572 30 5
ISBN (Paperback): 1 874572 40 2

Thanks: Natasha Briant, Rose Briant, Honor Conway, Roy Fielden, Alan George, Heather Godwin, Adam Green, Maria Harlan, Patrick Irwin, Alistair Jolly, Sue Jex, Herbert Levy, Hervıg Maehler, Nicolas Rollason, Nicolas Soames, Duncan Steen, Winfried Wartenberg.

Origination and Reprographics by Ads, St Albans, Hertfordshire
Printed by Redwood Books, Trowbridge, Wiltshire

CONTENTS

ILLUSTRATIONS

INTRODUCTION

It is a sad fact that letter writing is in decline. The telephone and other faster and easier methods of communication have made us lazy. There is, for example, the fashion for sending picture postcards or 'notelets' which only leave a minimum amount of space for the written message. A card for any event can now be purchased, such as "Congratulations on passing your driving test," or even, "Sorry to hear you're getting a divorce." Letters abroad are, more often than not, written on special, folding, air-mail forms, with stamp included, leaving little room to write expansively. Business letters and letters of confirmation are still current practice (as a tangible record of agreement), but the days of long newsy accounts are receding.

However, some people will always write letters, to be stored away by a few of the recipients and to be found later in attics and desks giving us a glimpse of another world. Reading a letter which is not intended for you is like eavesdropping. One only has to read a letter and straightway one is transported to that particular age and situation by being put directly in touch with both the sender and the receiver.

Letters provide hard evidence that events and customs took place in the way that historians have described them. Letters also provide the colour and the details often missing from other more official, less personal documentation. They contain words written at the time giving opinions, passions, fads and prejudices.

This book concentrates on letters between parents and their children. It covers a wide time-scale (130 B.C. – late 20th Century) and the letters are from a variety of sources. Included in this selection is correspondence from young children, courtiers, kings, queens, scientists, engineers, musicians, soldiers and adventurers as well as professional writers but all of them are writing as either a parent or a child. Many of the correspondents write as adult children to their parents and of course the relationship changes according to age.

Each letter, or sequence of letters, tells a story. Sometimes the story is of high drama but more often it is merely a small domestic tale, not, as Sir Walter Scott would call it, "the Big Bow-Wow". The subject matter does not change much through the centuries. The same themes recur over and over again – the expression of disappointment, ambition, requests for money, advice sought and advice given. Often letters are written because the writer cannot bring himself to tell something to a person's face. (G.K. Chesterton couldn't tell his mother face to face that he had become engaged to be married. He had to write a letter, even though they lived in the same house!)

Some of the letters are about the correspondents' professions. For example, the Stephensons, father and son, correspond in great technical detail about their engineering projects. They talk as equals enjoying being able to share their skills. Mozart shares with his father his musical opinions and problems. His father values his judgement in this field, though he firmly reserves the right to advise his son how to conduct his life and issues reprimands from time to time. Artists write of the importance of pursuing what they know they are impelled to do but what often their parents are afraid of; and soldiers try to explain war to families who, before the days of newspapers and fast communications, have no concept of what it must be like.

Some accomplished letter-writers were writing not only direct, personal letters to their parents or children, but, in the back of their minds were thinking of a wider public. It is quite likely that some were only too aware that their letters would be a valued addition to their 'oeuvres': Ernest Hemingway admitted that letters were a 'warming-up process'. A few letters are included in this collection because they not only illuminate the relationship, but because they are also well constructed or interesting pieces in their own right.

However, the main intention of this collection is to throw light on the relationship between parent and child and the letters have been chosen to reflect this. For example, in spite of all her preoccupation with affairs of state, Queen Victoria still found time to writer to her daughter about the small details of the upbringing of children and the behaviour of the young. We are shown a different side of the curmudgeonly queen – a mother who has firm ideas on discipline, yet who worries that she might have unintentionally upset her little grandson.

Letters written between parent and child are different from other types of letters. Whatever happens, parent and child are for ever emotionally entwined. They may not necessarily love each other, feelings may be one-sided, one party may be angry, the relationship may be strained; but if they are bothering to write, there must be some feeling – even if it is only perceived as duty. In the case of Sir Thomas More, his feeling towards his daughter, Margaret, is of the deepest love. His last letter to her written shortly before his execution reveals the depths that a parent's love for his child can go. Others, such as Scott Fitzgerald, choose to show their love in a more flippant manner while some parents appear to be only exasperated by their offspring – as is seen when Mrs Delius writes to her extravagant son, Fritz. On the children's side we read letters written out of duty, letters written containing confessions and frequent letters requesting funds. Plus ça change! People will always love, suffer, have ambitions, hopes and fears and it is hoped that this collection of letters taps this vast range of emotions between parents and children that stretches across centuries, nationalities and classes.

Human nature may be constant, but attitudes and preoccupations *do* change and relationships between parents and children have changed too. We, in the 20th century in the Western World, are normally very attached to our offspring. We often hear of someone confessing that his or her children are the mainspring of their lives. These days most parents are able to be involved in their children's lives – their aspirations, their problems, their successes and failures. They hope for so much, often wanting them to achieve what they themselves were not able to. Indeed, some children spend most of their lives trying to shake off their suffocating parents. In earlier centuries and amongst the middle and working classes, there simply wasn't the time for that amount of involvement. Essential work was more important and in addition parents expected at least one of their children to die and consequently invested less, emotionally, in a child. There was a more matter-of-fact approach to death. Life was often a struggle and as soon as children were old enough they would be sent out to work or married off and then regarded as independent. Not that this meant that they were then ignored or forgotten: but in that age children were forced to grow up and gain their independence more quickly than in the second half of this century.

Letters from parents to their children written in the Middle Ages show affection and duty. Nevertheless the main preoccupation was not an out-pouring of emotion but a concern with practicalities such as fixing the barn, reporting on property, requesting lengths of cloth and news about the livestock. Theirs was a materialistic society, but materialistic for a purpose – survival. Margaret Paston wrote reminding her son of repairs that needed doing on the estate because that was their family business and she was in charge after the death of her husband. Many of the letters from the children of this period to their parents were begging favours, such as the requests from the Lisle children that their parents should put in words for them to secure a good position at Court. Not many expressed homesickness or love.

By and large the early letters included in this collection are written by the literate and the land-owning class. It was this class which produced the educated and wealthy offspring and often these were the children to leave the country for the cities where they would lead public or private lives. With the Industrial Revolution came the growth of leisure when these individuals were not so concerned about eking out a living and could take the time to explore other pastimes. The middle classes found time to write letters and diaries and pursue hobbies. Until then, this had been the privilege of the gentry.

The importance of 'duty' both on the part of the parent and the child has always been apparent in letters but with Lord Chesterfield, in the mid–eighteenth century, it became a way of life. He pursued his duty to educate his illegitimate son in the correct way with a religious zeal. He wrote hundreds of letters which were later published as a handbook of etiquette. It is interesting to ponder on what his son, Philip, thought about the letters. He must have realized they were worth saving.

Parents in the latter half of this century are taught the importance of childhood experiences on future relationships. The responsibility and the effect that we have upon our children is drummed into us through books, education, television and even advertising. Sigmund Freud's teachings on the significance of the relationship between parents and children has had a profound influence on 20th Century thinking. An interesting letter from Anna Freud to her father is included in this collection in which she makes a conscious effort to analyse her feelings towards her father and the effect he had on her. She challenges her father's opinions in a way that would be unthinkable for a young daughter in the fifteenth to eighteenth centuries.

It seems a comparatively modern phenomenon to be so close to our children; to treat them as equals and confide in them. Today one often hears the remark, "they were like sisters" when describing a mother and daughter. This state of affairs would be very rare in the fifteenth to the nineteenth centuries, although there were exceptions. It is commonplace nowadays to examine our feelings, to search for our subconscious thoughts and motives and this trend is reflected in the letters of Sylvia Plath, to her mother. Feelings would be a low priority for the Paston or Lisle family.

Because of this development of attitudes, the letters are printed chronologically, which makes it easier to pick out changing patterns of behaviour and attitudes between parents and children. It is hoped that the collection tells a broad story, within which is contained a series of mini-tales, highlighting the similarities and the differences across the centuries.

It has already been said that this century has seen a decline in letter-writing and an increasing dependence on the telephone. For many children away at boarding school or summer camp, the weekly phone-call has replaced the weekly letter. Many parents will have experienced the perpetually busy college or university telephone and it is easier for the young traveller, taking a year off and trekking round the world, to phone home to report that they are alive or short of money, rather than write a letter. Lawrence of Arabia or Freya Stark would have been horrified. For them, to write letters was to make an important record of the strange sights they had seen whilst still maintaining the distance between home and their personal voyage of discovery. On the other hand, it is quite easy to imagine that Madame de Sévigné would have enjoyed picking up the telephone in Paris and dialling Provence to give her daughter the gossip about the city's society as quickly as possible.

A collection of this sort becomes even more interesting as the habit of letter-writing dwindles. Future historians will have a bleaker time trying to piece together the fragments of our time. Perhaps facsimile machines will lead to a return of letter writing – the modern equivalent of George Bernard Shaw's postcards in the long-gone era when communication by letter was important and there were three or four postal deliveries a day.

THE ANCIENT WORLD

130 B.C. – 4TH CENTURY A.D.

This anthology begins with a selection of letters between parents and their children of Ancient Greece and Egypt. The fact that so many are available to us may seem surprising given that the number of letters of the Middle Ages found in Europe is so small. The reason is two-fold. First, the letters were written on papyrus which remained well-preserved in the dry sand and thus protected from the ravages of weather and battle. Secondly, the Greeks and Egyptians had an advanced educational system. Temples usually had their own schools where the priests taught children to read and write and wealthy families employed tutors who taught the children to write in Greek. By the second century A.D. schools had been established with teachers salaried by the state. Reading and writing was taught at primary school and then, if the children were not needed to work for their parents, they were sent to secondary school. If a student wished to study to become a doctor, lawyer or teacher, he had to go to university, perhaps in Alexandria, the second city of the Ancient World. This entailed living far away from home and so letter-writing became an important means of communication.

Several of the following letters are from fathers or older sons written whilst serving in the army as well as from children studying away from home. Some convey great confidence, some concern for affairs at home and some hint at homesickness. One young student, for example, poignantly asks that his pigeons should be looked after.

The papyrus was made from reed-like grasses, one layer laid horizontally with another placed vertically on top. They were then weighted and pressed together, oozing a sticky resin, which gave the papyrus durability. The result was a tough cloth-like paper which has endured for two thousand years. The papyrus sheets were made to a standard size and then glued together as a roll for sale in Paper Shops. The standard roll was 20 sheets and a customer would buy whatever length he needed.

The ink was made from soot mixed with water and remains black and legible today; the pen was made from a reed.

Once written, letters were rolled up and tied with a piece of reed or thread. The address was written on the outside of the scroll which was

1

given to a messenger to deliver. Such was the sophistication of Egypt that a governmental postal service was developed for the distribution of official letters. It was only natural that ordinary people should take advantage of this and ask that their personal letters be included in the post-bag.

ESTHLADAS
130 B.C.

A letter written in Greek from Esthladas, probably in the army, to his parents.

Esthladas to his father and mother greeting and good health. As I have often written to you to keep a stout heart and take care of yourself until things settle down, once again please exhort yourself and our dependants to take courage. For news has come that Paos is sailing up in the month of Tubi with abundant forces to subdue the mobs at Hermonthis and deal with them as rebels. Look after my sisters also and Pelops and Stachys and Senathuris. Goodbye. Year 40, Choiach 23 (Addressed) Deliver at Pathyris to my father.

"The mobs at Hermonthis" is a reference to the conflict between Euergetes II, and his sister Cleopatra. Paos was the king's general.

LUCIUS BELLENUS GEMELLUS
100 A.D.

From a discharged veteran, Lucius Bellenus Gemellus to his son Sabinus. Gemellus owned land at Dionysias and other villages in the Fayrum.

Lucius Bellenus Gemellus to his son Sabinus greeting. On receipt of my letter you will kindly send me Pindarus, the field-guard at Dionysias, to the city, as Hermonax has asked me to let him take him to Kerkesoucha to examine his olive-grove, as it is too dense and he wishes to cut down some of the trees, in order that those to be cut down may be cut skilfully. And send the fish on the 24th or 25th for Gemella's birthday feast. Now do not talk nonsense about gathering your olives. Goodbye.

The 4th year of the Emperor Caesar Nerva Trajanus Augustus Germanicus, Choiak 18.

APOLLINARIUS
2ND CENTURY A.D.

From a recruit in Italy.

Apollinarius to Taesis, his mother and lady, many greetings. Before all I pray for your health. I myself am well and make supplication of you before the gods of this place. I wish you to know, mother, that I arrived in Rome in good health on the 25th of the month Pachon and was posted to Misenum, though I have not yet learned the name of my company; for I had not gone to Misenum at the time of writing this letter. I beg you then, mother, look after yourself and do not worry about me; for I have come to a fine place. Please write me a letter about your welfare and that of my brothers and of all your folk. And whenever I find a messenger I will write to you; never will I be slow to write. Many salutations to my brothers and Apollinarius and his children and Karalas and his children. I salute Ptolemaeus and Ptolemais and her children and Heraclous and her children. I salute all who love you, each by name. I pray for your health. (Addressed) Deliver at Karanis to Taesis, from her son Apollinarius of Misenum.

ANTONIUS LONGUS
2ND CENTURY A.D.

From a penitent son. This letter has been widely quoted as an illustration of the parable of the prodigal son. It is addressed to 'Nilous his mother from Antonius Longus her son.'

Antonius Longus to Nilous his mother very many greetings. I pray always for your health; every day I make supplication for you before the lord Serapis. I would have you know that I did not expect that you were going up to the metropolis; for that reason I did not come to the city myself. I was ashamed to come to Karanis, because I go about in filth. I wrote to you that I am naked. I beg you, mother, be reconciled to me. Well I know what I have brought on myself. I have received a fitting lesson. I know that I have sinned. I heard from . . . . who found you in the Arsinoite nome, and he has told you everything correctly. Do you not know that I would rather be maimed than feel that I still owe a man an obol?

SEMPRONIUS
2ND CENTURY A.D.

Sempronius to Saturnila, his mother and lady, very many greetings. Before everything I pray for your health and that of my brothers, unharmed by the evil eye, and withal I make supplication for you daily before the lord Serapis. How many letters have I sent you and not one have you written me in reply, though so many people have sailed down! I beg you, my lady, be not slow to write me news of your welfare that I may live in less anxiety; for your welfare is what I pray for always.

THONIS
EARLY 3RD CENTURY A.D.

Another son begging for news, this time from son to father.

To my lord and father Arion from Thonis greeting.

. . . . Look you, this is my fifth letter to you, and you have not written to me except only once, not even a word about your welfare, nor come to see me; though you promised me saying "I am coming," you have not come to find out whether the teacher is looking after me or not. He himself is inquiring about you almost every day, saying "Is he not coming yet?" And I just say "Yes."

He finishes by saying in a postscript,

"Remember our pigeons."

APOLLO
3RD CENTURY A.D. OR 4TH CENTURY A.D.

TO APOLLO FROM HIS SON

.... dearest father, and I pray to God that you are prosperous and successful and that we may receive you home in good health. I have indeed told you
before of my grief at your absence from among us, my fear being that something dreadful might happen to you and that we may not find your body.
Indeed I have often wished to tell you that in view of the unsettled state of
things I wanted to stamp a mark on you. . . .

> *It was customary to brand camels and other animals as a means of reclaiming
> them if stolen. In this case the writer's idea was that he should be able to iden-
> tify his father's body and give it proper burial.*

THEON
2ND CENTURY A.D.

Papyrus letter found at Oxyrhynchus.

Theon to his father Theon, greeting. It was a fine thing of you not to take
me with you to the city! If you won't take me with you to Alexandria I won't
write you a letter or speak to you or say goodbye to you; and if you go to
Alexandria I won't take you hand nor ever greet you again. That is what will
happen if you won't take me. Mother said to Archelaus, "It quite upsets him to
be left behind." It was good of you to send me presents . . . . on the 12th , the
day you sailed. Send me a letter, I implore you. If you don't, I won't eat, I
won't drink; there now!

MEDIAEVAL AND TUDOR WORLDS

1258–1540

LADY HAVISIA DE NEVILLE

C.1258

Lady Havisia de Neville's first husband, John de Neville, died in 1246. She later married Sir John Gatesden whom she refers to as her son's father-in-law.

Hugh de Neville, her son, was brought up at Windsor with other children of the nobility. He then participated in expeditions to Wales and Scotland and actively supported the Barons in the civil war. He had his possessions taken away in 1265 for the part he had played against Henry II but in 1266 he was pardoned, his lands were restored to him and later in the year Hugh went to the Holy Land, appointing his mother and brother as attorneys to oversee his property during his absence. At this time England was in a state of agitation with many young men of standing, such as Hugh de Neville, leaving the country to follow the Crusades. This meant that their monies were tied up and unobtainable, often when needed desperately. This is the background to Lady Neville's letter to her son.
(Written in French)

Havisia de Neville to her very dear son, Hugh de Neville, wished health and the blessing of God and her own.

Know, dear son, that I am well and hearty, thanks to God, and am much rejoiced at the news that William FitzSimon brought me of your health. God be thanked for it! Know, dear son, that our necessities of receiving the returns from your lands can avail nothing, on account of the great rule your adversary has in the king's court, unless you yourself were present. Wherefore your father-in-law and I, and all your other friends, agree that you should come to England, and we pray and entreat you, by the faith and love that you owe us, that you will not by any means fail in this; since you ought once again to return. For we know well that it would be a very great dishonour and we consider it a great sin, to suffer us and ours to be disinherited by your indolence. Therefore I anxiously pray you, dear son, that you will travel with all possible haste, and also, according to the counsel of all your friends, that you got to the court of Rome, and procure if you can the letter of the Pope, express and stringent, to the king of England, that he should restore your lands, and have them restored. And that you may make a proper understanding at the court of all our needs, without omitting or concealing anything; that is, how you are placed with the king, and that you are compelled by a writing to hold the (obligation), without contradiction and without ever making an acquisition to the contrary. For wise persons have said the acquisition would be worth nothing, unless it made express mention of this, that it was through no fault of yours that you made this the aforesaid obligation when in war, and through fear of prison.

And know, good son, that the first acquisition you got at Rome for our lands was not such as you understood, for it was only a loving petition for your rights of the money which you ought to have had of the crusade allowance. The legate, thanks to him, has granted us that he would let us have it if we could espy out where it is, but we have not as yet found any, except what is in the hands of such as themselves would wish to go into the Holy Land; but as much as we may be able to acquire now or henceforth, between this and St. John's day, we will then send you by the messengers of the Temple, who will bring their own money. And for God's sake, good son, guard against making such an obligation as you have made for Sir Ingelram de Umfranville; for I was grieved that it was proper to have it paid from our own demesne. And good, sweet, dear son, I anxiously pray you that you will send us word how much money you have really had by my command, for the thing is not in my power, for I could never spy a man who went to that part, that I might send you letters, that weighs no little upon me. For if it could be that I could often have good news of you, and comfort you again often by my messages, there would be nothing that could more rejoice me, expect it were to see and speak to you. And know, dear son, that my heart is grieved and alarmed day and night, since William FitzSimon brought me news that you were so poorly provided with money; but God who is Almighty, if it please him, give you speedy amendment, and I will do it to my utmost power.

Dear son, I pray you not to trust too much to the money of the crusade allowance, for they say that more great lords of England will take the cross; and they will take away as much as shall be raised for the crusade, as certain friends have given me to know. But do not ever cease, as you dearly love me, for no waiting for money, to borrow all the money that you can, and to go to the court of Rome to acquire for our necessities, and to hasten to come to England to accomplish our needs. For I hope, by the help of God, if you could well accomplish what you have to do about the acquisition of our lands, that you will see such change in England, that never in our time could you have better accomplished your wish, or more to your honour. Wherefore cease not to solicit again about your coming, since you can here best serve God. I commend you to the true body of God, who give you life and health. Sir Walter de la Hide, Joanna your sister, and all our household, salute you. And know, dear son, that my counsel is that you obtain the letters of request of the legate of that country, and the letters of the master of the Temple and of the Hospital, to the legate of England and to other rich men, for your needs, and in testimony of your deeds in that country on the occasion of your coming. And ever take care of your house that you have there, if God give you courage to return.

ELEANOR QUEEN-DOWAGER OF ENGLAND
DIED 1291

In this letter written to her son, Edward I, we have a rare indication of the love that existed between parents and their offspring, despite the tendency for children of the ruling classes to be brought up by others outside the immediate family from an early age.

To the most noble prince and her very dear son, Edward, by God's grace King of England, Lord of Ireland, and Duke of Aquitaine, Eleanora, humble nun of the order of Fontevraud, of the convent of Amesbury, wishes health and her blessing.

Sweetest son, we know well how great is the desire that a mother has to see her child when she has been long away from him, and that dame Margaret de Nevile, companion of Master John Giffard, has not seen for a long time past her child, who is in the keeping of dame Margaret de Weyland, and has a great desire to see him. We pray you, sweetest son, that you will command and pray the aforesaid Margaret de Weyland, that she will suffer that the mother may have the solace of her child for some time, after her desire. Dearest son, we commend you to God. Given at Amesbury, the 4th day of March.

EDWARD II
1284-1327

In 1324 war broke out between England and France. Edward II sent his wife, Isabella of France, to negotiate a treaty with her brother, the French King, Charles IV. Her marriage with Edward II was not a happy one. Edward II was a cruel and unsuitable husband as well as being an incompetent monarch. Whilst ostensibly negotiating a peace, Isabella was actually building up support for her own cause. She had taken a lover and wanted her son to join her. So she persuaded Edward II to send Edward, Prince of Wales to France in order to pay homage to the French King on his father's behalf.

The following letter was written by King Edward II to the Prince of Wales after his departure for France. King Edward II was uneasy about what was happening and urged his son "to tear himself away from the evil counsels by which he was surrounded".

(Written in French) 1326

Edward, fair son,

We have seen, by your letters lately written to us, that you well remember the charges we enjoined you on your departure from Dover, and that you have not transgressed our commands in any point that was in your power to avoid. But to us it appears that you have not humbly obeyed our commands as a good son ought his father, since you have not returned to us, to be under government, as we have enjoined you by our other letters, on our blessing, but have notoriously held companionship, and your mother, also, with Mortimer, our traitor and mortal enemy, who, in company with your mother and others, was publicly carried to Paris in your train, to the solemnity of the coronation, at Pentecost just past, in signal despite of us, and to the great dishonour both of us and you; for truly he is neither a meet companion for your mother nor for you, and we hold that much evil to the country will come of it.

Also, we understand that you, through counsel, which is contrary both to our interest and yours, have proceeded to make divers alterations, injunctions, and ordinances, without our advice, and contrary to our orders, in the Duchy of Guienne, which we have given you; but you ought to remember the conditions of the gift, and your reply when it was conferred upon you at Dover. These things are inconvenient, and must be most injurious. Therefore, we command and charge you, on the faith and love you ought to bear us, and on our blessing, that you show yourself our dear and well-beloved son, as you have aforetime done; and ceasing from all excuses of your mother, or any like those that you have just written, you come to us here with all haste, that we may ordain for you and your estates as honourably as you can desire.

By right and reason, you ought to have no other governor than us, neither should you wish to have.

Also, fair son, we charge you by no means to marry till you return to us, nor without our advice and consent, nor for any cause either go to the Duchy, or elsewhere, against our will and command.

PS. Edward, fair son, you are of tender age; take our commandments tenderly to heart and so rule your conduct with humility, as you would escape our reproach, our grief, and indignation, and advance your own interest and honour. Believe no counsel that is contrary to the will of your father, as the wise King Solomon instructs you. Understand certainly, that if you now act contrary to our counsel, and continue in wilful disobedience, you will feel it all the days of your life, and all other sons will take example to be disobedient to their lords and fathers.

THE PASTON LETTERS
1440–1504

The Paston Letters are a collection of letters written in the 15th and 16th Centuries, mostly by or to, members of the Norfolk family of Paston. The family took their name from the village where they lived, about 20 miles from Norwich, on the north-east coast of the county. They were an educated family of wealth and property and very influential in East Anglia.

These are amongst the earliest surviving private letters in English and are mostly about the running of the estate and worries and concerns with

regard to the behaviour of the children and their financial situation.
William Paston I was born in 1378, son of Clement Paston. He was
the Steward of the Duke of Norfolk and a J.P. In 1420 he married Agnes
Berry and held various important public positions. He died in 1444
leaving his wife, with the help of her sons, to run the estate.

Agnes was the daughter and heiress of Sir Edmund Berry of
Horwellbury near Royston, Herts. She lived mostly in Norfolk either at
Paston or Oxnead but for some years before her death in 1479, she lived
with her son, William, in London. Agnes had five children and she
often wrote to them when they were grown up and away from home,
especially to her two elder sons. Her letters to her absent sons show her
to be a domineering and capable widow.

John Paston I, the eldest son, was born in 1421 and followed his
father into the law. He married Margaret, who came to him from a
wealthy and educated family and they lived in Paston. However, he
spent a great deal of his time away trying to establish his claim to
Caistor Castle and numerous manors in Norfolk. Whilst he was away
and after the death of his mother, Margaret took charge of the running
of the estates.

Edmund also studied law but died at the early age of 24.

AGNES PASTON TO EDMUND PASTON I

4 February 1445

To mine well beloved son, I greet you well, and advise you to think once
of the day of your father's counsel to learn the law; for he said many times that
whosoever should dwell at Paston should need to con defend himself.

The vicary of Paston and your father, in Lentern last was, were through
and accorded, and doles set out how broad the way should been: and now he
hath pulled up the doles and saith he will maken a ditch fro the corner of his
wall right over the way to the new ditch of the great close. And there is a man
in Trunch hight Palmer too, that had of your grandfather certain land in
Trunch on seven year or eight year agone for corn, and truly hath paid all the
years; and now he hath suffered the corn to be withset for 8s. of rent to
Gimingham, which your father paid never. Geoffrey asked Palmer why the
rent was not asked in mine husband's time; and Palmer said, for he was a great
man, and a wise man of the law, and that was the cause men would not ask
him the rent . . . .

I send you not this letter to make you weary of Paston, for I live in hope,
and ye will learn that they shall be made weary of their work; for in good faith

I dare well sayn it was your father's last will to have do right well to that place, and that I can show of good proof, though men would say nay.

God make you right good a man, and send God's blessing and mine. Written in haste at Norwich the Thursday after Candlemas Day.

Weeteth of your brother John how many joists will serve the parlour and the chapel at Paston, and what length they must be and what brede and thickness they must be; for your father's last will was, as I ween verily, that they should be 9 inches one way and 7 another way. And purveyeth therefor that they mow be squared there and sent hither, for here can none such be had in this country. And say to your brother John it were well done to think on Stanstead church. And I pray you to send me tidings from beyond sea, for here they arn afeared to tell such as be reported.

By your mother, Agnes Paston

AGNES PASTON TO JOHN PASTON I

6 July 1453

. . . . I pray you that ye will pay your William for four onces and a half of silk as he paid, which he sent me by William Taverner and bring with you a quarter of an ounce even like of the same that I send you closed in this letter. And say your brother William that his horse has a farcin and great running sores in his legs.

God have you in keeping. Written at Norwich on Saint Thomas' Even in great haste.

By your mother, A. Paston

Elizabeth was William and Agnes Paston's only daughter and was born after Edmond in 1429. She married Robert Poynings in 1458 at the comparatively advanced age of 29 years. In this letter to her mother she is anxious that the promised £120 which is part of her inheritance and owed to her husband should be paid quickly. It sounds a dutiful marriage rather than one of love.

ELIZABETH POYNINGS TO AGNES PASTON

3 January 1459

Right worshipful and my most entirely beloved mother, in the most lowly manner I recommend me unto your good motherhood, beseeching you daily and nightly of your motherly blessing; evermore desiring to hear of your welfare and prosperity, the which I pray God to continue and increase to your heart's desire. And if it liked your good motherhood to hear of me and how I do, at the making of this letter I was in good heal of body, thanked be to Jesu.

And as for my master, my best-beloved that ye call, and I must needs call him so now, for I find none other cause, and as I trust to Jesu never shall; for he is full kind unto me, and is as busy as he can to make me sure of my join-ture, whereto he is ibound in a bond of £1000 to you, mother, and to my brother William, and to Edmund Clere, the which needed no such bond. Wherefore I beseech you, good mother, as our most singular trust is in your good mother-hood, that my master, my best-beloved, fail not of the 100 mark at the beginning of this term, the which ye promised him to his marriage, with the remnant of the money of my father's will. For I have promised faithfully to a gentleman called Bain, that was one of my best-beloved sureties and was bound to him in £200, of which he rehearseth for to receive at the beginning of this term £120; and if he fail thereof at this time he will claim the whole of us the which were to make us too great an hurt. And he cannot make an end with none of his other sureties without this said silver, and that can my brother John tell you well enough an it lusteth him to do so.

And Jesu for his great mercy save you. Written at London the Wednesday the 3 day of January.

By your humble daughter, Elizabeth Poynings

After Agnes' death the estate passed to John Paston I and whilst he was away he left his very capable wife to look after its affairs. John and Margaret had seven children and Margaret wrote frequently to them, particularly after her husband's death in 1484. This letter to her eldest son John, however, is written before his death and is a typical mother's letter rebuking her son for leaving home without her knowledge and consent, though in order to keep the peace Margaret is happy to let her husband think otherwise. This is a matter between her and her son and she is writing without her husband's knowledge. She also charges him to live within his income.

MARGARET PASTON TO JOHN PASTON II

15 November 1463

I greet you well, and send you God's blessing and mine, letting you know wit that I have received a letter from you the which ye delivered to Master Roger at Lynn, whereby I conceive that ye think did not well that ye departed hence without my knowledge. Wherefore I let you wit I was right evil paid with you. Your father thought, and thinketh yet, that I was assented to your departing, and that hath caused me to have great heaviness. I hope he will be your good father hereafter, if ye demean you well and do as ye owe to do to him; and I charge you upon my blessing that in anything touching your father that should be his worship, profit, or avail that ye do your devoir and diligent labour to the furtherance therein, as ye will have my good will; and that shall cause your father to be better father to you.

I was told me ye sent him a letter to London. What the intent thereof I wot not, but though he took it but lightly, I would ye should not spare to write to him again as lowly as ye can, beseeching him to be your good father, and send him such tidings as beth in the country there ye beth in; and that ye beware of your expense better (than) ye have be before this time, and be your own purse-bearer. I trow ye shall find it most profitable to you.

I would ye should send me word how ye do, and how ye have chevished for yourself sin ye departed hence, by some trusty man, and that your father have no knowledge thereof. I durst not let him know of the last letter that ye wrote to me, because he was so sore displeased with me at that time.

. . . . Written at Caister the Tuesday next before Saint Edmund the King.

Your mother, M. Paston

I would ye should make much of the parson (of) Filby, the bearer hereof, and make him good cheer if ye may.

KING HENRY VII
1457–1509

Henry was the son of Edmund Tudor, Earl of Richmond, and Margaret Beaufort, the grand-daughter of John of Gaunt and heiress of the House of Lancaster. During Henry's childhood he and his mother were never separated and Margaret had much to do with his marriage to Elizabeth of York, the heiress of the House of Plantagenet, realizing how formidable a union between York and Lancaster would be. In the following letter, Henry – King of England for many years – still respects his mother's opinions and advice.

c.1498

Madame, my most entirely Well-beloved Lady and Mother,

I recommend me unto you in the most humble and lowly wise that I can, beseeching you of your daily and continual blessings.

By your confessor, the bearer, I have received your good and most loving writing . . . . I shall be as glad to please you as your heart can desire it, and I know well that I am as much bounden so to do as any creature living, for the great and singular motherly love and affection that it hath pleased you at all times to bear towards me. Wherefore mine own most loving Mother, in my most hearty manner I thank you, beseeching you of your good continuance of the same.

And, madame, your said confessor hath moreover shown unto me, on your behalf, that ye, of your goodness and kind disposition, have given and granted unto me such title and interest as ye have – or ought to have – in such debts and duties which are owing and due unto you in France by the French king and others: wherefore, madame, in my most hearty and humbel wise, I thank you. Howbeit, I verily think it will be right hard to recover it [the title] without it being driven by compulsion and force – rather than by any true justice – which is not yet, as we think any convenient time to be put into execution . . . .

And verily, madame, an I might recover it at this time, or any other, ye be sure ye should have your pleasure therein, as I – and all that God has given me – am, and ever shall be, at your will and commandment, as I have instructed Master Fisher more largely herein, as I doubt not he will declare unto you. And I beseech you to send me your mind and pleasure in the same, which I shall be full glad to follow, with God's grace, the which send and give unto you the full accomplishment of all your noble and virtuous desires.

Written at Greenwich, the 17th day of July, with the hand of your most humble and loving son,

H.R.

. . . . Madame, I have encumbered you now with this long writing, but think that I can do no less, considering that it is so seldom that I do write, wherefore I beseech you to pardon me: for verily, madame, my sight is nothing so perfect as it has been, and I know well it will appayre daily, wherefore I trust that you will not be displeased, though I write not so often with mine own hand, for on my faith I have been three days or I could make an end of this letter.

SIR THOMAS MORE
1478–1535

The eminent scholar and respected politician, author of *Utopia* and Chancellor under Henry VIII, was a great family man who filled his home with books, friends and interesting conversation. In this extract from his Latin verses Sir Thomas More greets his children, Margaret, Elizabeth, Cecilia and John. It was probably written in 1517 when he went to Calais and the children were still young. It is a finely constructed piece of renaissance writing intended more as an emotional expression of his great love than an actual letter to his offspring.

I hope that a letter to all of you may find my four children in good health and that your father's good wishes may keep you so. In the meantime, while I make a long journey, drenched by a soaking rain, and while my mount, too frequently, is bogged down in the mud, I compose these verses for you in the hope that, although unpolished, they may give you pleasure. From them you may gather an indication of your father's feelings for you – how much more than his own eyes he loves you; for the mud, miserably stormy weather, and necessity for driving a diminutive horse through deep waters have not been able to distract his thoughts from you or to prevent his proving that, wherever he is, he thinks of you. For instance, when and it is often – his horse stumbles and threatens to fall, your father is not interrupted in the composition of his verses. Poetry often springs from a heart which has no feeling; these verses a father's love provides – along with a father's natural anxiety. It is not so strange that I love you with my whole heart, for being a father is not a tie which can be ignored. Nature in her wisdom has attached the parent to the child and bound them spiritually together with a Herculean knot. This tie is the source of my consideration for your immature minds, a consideration which causes me to take you often into my arms. This tie is the reason why I regularly fed you cake and gave you ripe apples and pears. This tie is the reason why I used to dress you in silken garments and why I never could endure to hear you cry. You know, for example, how often I kissed you, how seldom I whipped you. My whip was invariably a peacock's tail. Even this I wielded hesitantly and gently so that sorry welts might not disfigure your tender seats. Brutal and unworthy to be called father is he who does not weep himself at the tears of his child. How other fathers act I do not know, but you know well how gentle and devoted is my manner towards you, for I have always profoundly loved my own children and I have always been an indulgent parent – as every father ought to be. But at this moment my love has increased so much that it seems to me I used not to to love you at all. This feeling of mine is produced by your adult manners, adult despite your tender years; by your instincts, trained in noble principles which must be learned; by your pleasant way of speaking, fashioned for clarity; and by your very careful weighing of every word. These characteristics of yours so strangely tug at my heart, so closely bind me to you, my children, that my being your father (the only reason for many a father's love) is hardly a reason at all for my love of you. Therefore, most dearly beloved children all, continue to endear yourselves to your father and, by those same accomplishments which make me think that I had not loved you before, make me think hereafter (for you can do it) that I do not love you now.

> Sir Thomas More wrote the following letter to his eldest daughter Margaret from the Tower of London with a piece of coal, on 5 July 1535. He had been imprisoned over the question of the King's "great matter", this being the question of the King's divorce from Catherine of Aragon and proposed re-marriage. More was martyred for his faith on Tower Hill. Soon after, his son-in-law William Roper wrote his *Life* on Sir Thomas More (though he did not dare publish it until 20 years after More's death) and described his wife's last visit to see her father in order to obtain his blessing:

"When Sir Thomas More came from Westminster to the Tower-ward again, his daughter, my wife, desirous to see her father, whom she thought she should never see in this world after, and also to have his final blessing, gave attendance about the Tower Wharf, where she knew he should pass by, before he could enter into the Tower. There tarrying for his coming, as soon as she saw him, after his blessing upon her knees reverently received, she hasting towards him, and without consideration or care of herself, pressing in among the midst of the throng and company of the guard, that with halberds and bills went round about him, hastily ran to him, and there openly in the sight of them all, embraced him, took him about the neck and kissed him. Who well liking her most natural and dear daughterly affection towards him, gave her his fatherly blessing, and many godly words of comfort besides."

Sir Thomas More was particularly close to his eldest daughter. Margaret or Meg as he called her, received this letter from him on the eve of his death and William Roper included it in his *Life*.

I cumber you, good Margaret, much; but I would be sorry if it should be any longer than tomorrow. For tomorrow is Saint Thomas's Even and the Utas of Saint Peter; and therefore tomorrow long I to go to God. It were a day very and convenient for me, etc, I never liked your manner toward me better than when you kissed me last; for I love when daughterly love and dear charity hath no leisure to look for worldly courtesy. Farewell, my dear child, and pray for me, and I shall for you and all your friends, that we may merrily meet in heaven . . . .

THE LISLE LETTERS
1533–1540

Arthur Viscount Lisle, illegitimate son of Edward IV and as such the last of the Plantagenets, was appointed Governor of Calais by Henry VIII in 1533. He travelled there with his wife Honor to take up his post. Both had been married before, Arthur to Elizabeth Grey and Honor to John Basset, a west country nobleman. Between them they had no less than fourteen children and stepchildren, all treated as immediate family.

The letters, mainly to and from Honor Lisle, show a strong-willed natural organiser, busy obtaining favours to educate and advance her

Basset children. Anne and Mary she placed in respectable French homes to be "finished", while James was sent to follow a fashionable French education in Paris. Katherine sought to be a maid of honour to Henry VIII's Queen, and Honor succeeded in placing her with Lady Rutland, an oracle on court gossip. It was Anne, however, who was chosen as a maid, being the prettiest and wittiest of the daughters, and, having fallen under Henry's roving eye at court, she was tipped to be the next Queen.

Throughout the letters we see the practical nature of their lives (not unlike the Paston family writing three-quarters of a century before) and the system of rewarding favours with hunting dogs and birds, fine wines and quails, which Lord Lisle bred for this purpose. Above all, the letters provide us with a unique insight into the ambitions and workings of an upper-class sixteenth century family.

ANNE BASSET TO LADY LISLE

11 May 1534

. . . . Madame, and if it might please you, I would heartily desire you to send me some demi-worsted for a gown, and a kirtle of velvet, and also some linen to make smocks, and some hosen and shoes. I send you back again the gold ornaments which I brought with me, because I know not how to make use of them here. I heartily beseech you that it may please you to send me some others. I have need of three ells of red cloth to make me a cloak, with a hood of satin. . . .

Your most humble and very obedient daughter,

Anne Basset

ANNE BASSET TO LADY LISLE

17 August 1535

Madame, I commend me to your good favour as effectually and in the most humblest wise that I can.

Madame, I was very glad to receive good news of you, as also of the coming of my brother, whom Madame findeth handsome and of good conditions and that he knoweth enough to to converse. Madame, I would most earnestly entreat you that if I am to pass the winter in France I may have some gown to pass it in, as I am all out of apparel for every day. Madame, I know well that I am very costly unto you, but it is not possible to do otherwise, there are so many little trifling things which are here necessary which are not needed in England, and one must do as others do. Madame, I have received some shoes and some hosen which are too small for me: I beseech you of your goodness to send me some others. And thus I make an end, praying God to preserve you in health with prosperous and long life.

From Pont de Remy, the xvijth day of this month.

Entirely your humble and obedient daughter,

Anne Basset

MARY BASSET TO LADY LISLE

13 March 1536

Madame, I commend me most humbly to the good grace of my lord my father, and to yours. Madame, I am greatly rejoiced that Madame de Bours is sending you to know of your welfare. I most humbly thank you for the seven score pearls, and for the crown that it hath pleased you to send me. I send you a pair of knives for to put in your cabinet, because I think that you have none of such fashion. The spinet-player who taught me at Guechart Madame de Bours hath contented for that which he hath done; and she hath taken another in this town. Also, I have given the schoolmaster who taught me to read and write ten sols only, while waiting to hear from you. My said lady of Bours as yet hath not had my dress of satin mended, because to this hour she hath been right occupied with her affairs. She will have it repaired by Easter, and also will look about her to find some good spinet. I am greatly indebted to the said lady, who taketh always much pains for me. She doth not send you the items, what she hath spent for me; but when you shall send here one of your servants the sum thereof will be given him to bring you.. . . .

MARY BASSET TO LADY LISLE

23 December 1536

. . . . Madame, I most humbly beseech you that it will please you to pardon me that I have so many expenses to write you of: to make my peace with you I send you a little melon. I pray you to take it in gree. . . .

JAMES BASSET TO LADY LISLE

30 September 1537

My most honoured Mother, I recommend me to your good grace as effec-tually as I can, not forgetting my lord my father, my sisters and all my friends in those parts.

Madame, I have received your letters and the cramp rings, by the which I perceive the good affection you bear me is more and more augmented. As for your wish to have me learn the Latin tongue, for that it is the thing I most desire so that I may frequent the company of those who are stranger born and not only because it is your will for me I would for a year employ myself in the study thereof to the most of my power . . . .

From your very humble and obedient son,

James Basset

MARY BASSET TO LADY LISLE

17 March 1537

. . . . I pray that it may please our Lord to send you your heart's desire, with safe deliverance of your child, and that he may send you a good hour, even such a desire for you. If I might have my wish I would be with you when you shall be brought to bed, to warm his swaddling clouts for the babe. I have besought all my good friends to pray God for you, and chiefly I have com-mended you to the good prayers of my schoolmaster when he sayeth his mass, who recommendeth him to your good grace.

I pray our Creator, madame, to give you very good and long life.

From Abbeville, the xvijth of March.

Your obedient and very humble daughter,

Mary Basset

KATHERINE BASSET TO LADY LISLE

19 October 1539

. . . . Madame, the cause of my writing to your ladyship is, that we hear that the King's Grace shall be married, and my lord and lady as yet doth hear no word of their coming up to London. Wherefore I desire your ladyship that ye will be so good lady and mother unto me as to speak that I may be one of the Queen's maids; for I have no trust in none other than your ladyship to speak for me in that cause. . . .

And thus I pray Jesu preserve you in long life to His pleasure,
By your humble daughter,
Katherine Basset

LETTERS TO YOUNG SONS

1546–1641

KING EDWARD VI
1537–1553

The following is a translation of a letter, written in Latin, by Prince Edward (afterwards King Edward VI) to his father, King Henry VIII in 1546. He was 9 years old. For a period of time he shared lessons at Hatfield House with his half sister, the future Elizabeth I. They had some of the finest tutors in the land and were taught divinity, ancient and foreign languages as well as history, geography, mathematics, science and music. By the age of seven Edward wrote admirable Latin verse. The original of this letter is in the library of Hatfield House where Prince Edward wrote it.

If sons, in their loyalty, ought to honour their parents in every duty, I am quite old enough to realise that is is my duty to please Your Majesty in every way, not only because you are my father, but because you are a most devoted father and very fond of your son. Therefore, since I cannot yet fulfil any other duty to your good self except offering greeting, and that only by letter rather than in person, I have decided to write to you again. Moreover, I ask Your Highness to bestow your blessing on me. I am eager to see your Majesty, yet I do not press my request unduly, if it does not please Your Highness. Finally I pray to God and I wish that Your Majesty may enjoy a very long and happy life.

Your Majesty's most obedient son,
Prince Edward

SIR HENRY SIDNEY
1529-1586

Henry Sidney was Lord Deputy of Ireland and Lord President of Wales. His son, Philip (1554–1586) was the poet whose most notable works included *Arcadia*, *Defence of Poetry* and *Astrophel and Stella*. Philip attended Shrewsbury School and this letter from his father was written to him there. The post-script added by his mother underlines the closeness of the family and the tenderness felt for Philip.

1566

Son Philip

Have received two letters from you – one written in Latin, the other in French – which I take in good part; and will you to exercise that practice of learning often: for that will stand you most stead in that profession of life that you are born to live in.

And now sithence this is my first letter that ever I did write to you, I will not that it be all empty of some advices; which my natural care of you provoketh me to wish you to follow, as documents to you in this your tender age.

Let your first action be the lifting up of your mind to Almighty God by hearty prayer; and feelingly digest the words you speak in prayer, with continual meditation and thinking of Him to whom you pray: and use this as an ordinary act, and at an ordinary hour. Whereby the time itself will put you in remembrance to do that which you are accustomed to do in that time.

Apply your study such hours as your discreet Master doth assign you, earnestly: and the time, I know, he will so limit; as shall be both sufficient for your learning, and safe for your health. And mark the sense and matter of that you do read as well as the words: so shall you both enrich your tongue with words and your wit with matter; and judgment will grow as years grow in you.

Be humble and obedient to your Master: for unless you frame yourself to obey others, yea, and feel in yourself what obedience is; you shall never be able to teach others how to obey you. Be courteous of gesture and affable unto all men; with diversity of reverence according to the dignity of the person. There is nothing that winneth so much, with so little cost.

Use moderate diet: so as, after your meal, you may find your wit fresher, and not duller; and your body more lively, and not more heavy. Seldom drink wine; and yet sometimes do; lest being enforced to drink upon the sudden, you should find yourself inflamed.

Use exercise of body, but such as is without peril of your bones or joints. It will increase your force, and enlarge your breath. Delight to be cleanly as well in all parts of your body, as in your garments. It shall make you grateful in each company: and otherwise loathsome.

Give yourself to be merry: for you degenerate from your father, if you find not yourself most able in wit and body to do anything, when you be most merry. But let your mirth be ever void of all scurrility and biting words to any man: for a wound given by a word is oftentimes harder to be cured than that which is given with the sword.

Be you rather a hearer and bearer away of other men's talk, than a beginner or procurer of speech: otherwise you shall be accounted to delight to hear yourself speak.

Be modest in each assembly, and rather be rebuked of light fellows for maiden-like shamefastness; than of your sad (sober) friends, for pert boldness. Think upon every word that you will speak, before you utter it: and remember how Nature hath rampered (walled) up, as it were, the tongue with teeth, lips, yea, and hair without the lips; all, betokening reins or bridles for the loose use of that member.

Above all things, tell no untruth. No, not in trifles. The custom of it is nought: and let it not satisfy you that, for a time, the hearers take it for a truth: yet after it will be known as it is, to your shame. For there cannot be a greater reproach to a Gentleman, than to be accounted a liar.

Study and endeavour yourself to be virtuously occupied: so shall you make such an habit of well doing in you; as you shall not know how to do evil, though you would.

Remember, my son! the noble blood you are descended of by your mother's side: and think that only by virtuous life and good action you may be an ornament to that illustrious family; otherwise, through vice and sloth, you may be counted *labes generis*, "a spot of your kin," one of the greatest curses that can happen to man.

Well, my little Philip, this is enough for me; and too much, I fear, for you. But if I shall find that this light meat of digestion nourish in anything, the weak stomach of your young capacity; I will, as I find the same grow stronger, feed it with other food.

Commend me most heartily unto Master Justice Corbet, old Master

Onslowe, and my cousin his son. Farewell. Your mother and I send you our blessings: and Almighty God grant you His. Nourish you with His fear! govern you with His grace, and make you a good servant to your Prince and country!
Your loving father,
So long as you live in the fear of God,
H. Sydney.

A Postcript by my Lady Mary Sidney, in the skirts of my Lord President's letter, to her said son Philip.

Your noble and careful father hath taken pains with his own hand to give you in this his letter, so wise, so learned, and most requisite precepts for you to follow with a diligent and humble thankful mind; as I will not withdraw your eyes from beholding and reverent honouring the same: no, not so long time as to read any letter from me. And therefore, at this time, I will write unto you no other letter than this: whereby I first bless you, with my desire to God to plant in you His grace; and secondarily, warn you to have always before the eyes of your mind these excellent counsels of my lord you dear father, and that you fail not continually once in four or five days to read them over.

And for a final leave-taking for this time, see that you show yourself as a loving obedient scholar to your good Master, to govern you yet many years; and that my lord and I may hear that you profit so in your learning, as thereby you may increase our loving care of you, and deserve at his hands the continuance of his great joy, to have him often witness with his own hand the hope he hath in your well doing.

Farewell, my little Philip and once again the Lord bless you.
Your loving mother,
Mary Sidney.

JAMES I
1566–1625

James was the only child of Mary, Queen of Scots, by her second husband, Lord Henry Darnley. Fourteen months after his birth, Mary Stuart, having reigned some eight years, was forced to renounce her Crown in favour of her son. He was crowned at Stirling as James VI and James Stuart, Earl of Moray, became regent. James's succession to the English throne in 1603 brought the kingdoms of England and Scotland under one sovereign. His consort was Anne of Denmark and when he came to England to rule, he left her behind in Edinburgh, and his son and heir, Prince Henry, who was then 10 years old, at Stirling Castle, guarded by a strong garrison for fear of kidnap or murder. He sent him this letter shortly before setting out on his journey to England.

April 1603

My Son,

That I see you not before my parting, impute to this great occasion, wherein time is so precious; but that shall, by God's grace, be recompensed by your coming to me shortly, and continual residence with me ever after. Let not this news make you proud or insolent, for a king's son ye were, and no more are ye now; the augmentation that is hereby like to fall to ye, is but in cares and heavy burden. Be merry, but not insolent; keep a greatness, but *sine fastu*; be resolute, but not wilful; be kind, but in honourable birth; and, above all things, never give countenance to any, but as ye are informed they are in estimation with me.

Look upon all Englishmen that shall come to visit you as your loving subjects, not with ceremoniousness as towards strangers, but with that heartiness which at this time they deserve. This gentleman whom the bearer accompanies, is worthy, and of good rank, and now my family servitor; use him, therefore, in a more homely, loving sort than others.

I send ye herewith my book lately printed. Study and profit in it, as ye would deserve my blessing; and as there can nothing happen unto you whereof ye will not find the general ground therein, if not the particular point touched, so must ye level every man's opinions or advices with the rules there set down, allowing and following their advices that agree with the same, mistrusting and frowning upon them that advise ye to the contraire. Be diligent and earnest in your studies, that at your meeting with me I may praise ye for your progress in learning. Be obedient to your master for your own weal, and to procure my thanks; for in reverencing him, ye obey me and honour yourself. Farewell.

Your loving father,

James R.

The book that James I refers to is The Basilicon Doron, *or* His Majesty's Instructions to His dearest Son, the Prince. *The book at a later date was to be highly approved of by men of learning.*

HENRIETTA MARIA, QUEEN-CONSORT OF CHARLES I
1609–1669

Her first letter to her son, afterwards Charles II, was written when Henrietta Maria had heard from his guardian and tutor at Richmond Palace, the Earl of Newcastle, that the Prince of Wales was a difficult little patient, and had refused to take some nauseous medicine.

c. 1641

Charles,

I am sorry I must begin my first letter with chiding you, because I hear that you will not take physic. I hope it was only for this day, and that tomorrow you will do it; for if you will not, I must come to you and make you take it, for it is for your health.

I have given order to my Lord of Newcastle, to send me word tonight whether you will or not; therefore I hope you will not give the pain to come.

And so I rest

Your affectionate Mother,

Henrietta Marie

To my dear son, the Prince.

WOMEN OF INFLUENCE

1671–1689

MADAME DE SÉVIGNÉ
1626–1696

Marie de Rabutin Chantal or Madame de Sévigné, was a society woman, well read and well connected, who frequented the fashionable salons of seventeenth century Paris as well as the Court of Louis XIV. Amongst her closest acquaintances were Madame de La Fayette, author of La Princesse de Cleves and a leading light in the salon circuit, as well as Monsieur de la Rochefoucauld, one of the nobles who had rebelled against the monarchy in the mid-century civil wars. Other friends were the playwright, Corneille, and Madame de Maintenon, the King's mistress.

Madame de Sévigné, widowed at the age of 25, had been left with two children: Charles, who became a society playboy, and Françoise. It was her daughter's marriage to Monsieur de Grignan and their move to Provence, where he was Governor, which prompted her letters. She made up for her daughter's absence and relieved her sense of loss by writing to her almost daily. The letters show a mother, perhaps with too much time on her hands, over-concerned with her daughter's health and pregnancies. She also liked to nag the couple over their excessive spending. The letters are a blend of emotional outpouring, humour and gossip and they provided the provincial couple with invaluable news from the capital at a time when there were few newspapers. It is obvious from her output that Madame de Sévigné needed and enjoyed writing, regarding it as a diary which she kept almost daily.

TO MADAME DE GRIGNAN FROM HER MOTHER MADAME DE SÉVIGNÉ

Paris
Friday 6 February 1671

My affliction would be very ordinary if I could describe it to you, so I won't undertake it. I look in vain for my dear daughter, but can no longer find her, and her every step takes her further from me. So I went off to Sainte-Marie, still weeping, still lifeless. It seemed as if my heart and soul were being torn out of me, and truly, what a brutal separation! I asked to be free to be alone. I was taken into Mme. du Housset's room, where they lit a fire for me. Agnes looked at me but didn't speak; such was our understanding. I stayed there until five and never stopped sobbing; all my thoughts were killing me. I wrote to M. de Grignan, in what tone you can well imagine. I went on to Mme. de La Fayette's, and she intensified my grief by the sympathy she showed. She was alone and ill, and depressed about the death of one of her sisters who was a nun – in fact she was just as I would have wished her. M. de La Rochefoucauld came. We talked of nothing but you, of the justification I had for being upset and of his intention to speak severely to *Melusine*. I can tell you that she will be harried. D'Hacqueville will give you a good account of this affair. I came home eventually from Mme. de La Fayette's at eight, but coming in here, oh God! Can you imagine what I felt as I came up the stairs? That room where I always used to go – alas, I found the doors open but everything empty and in a muddle, and your poor little girl to remind me of my own. Can you understand all I went through? Black awakenings during the night, and in the morning I was not a step nearer finding rest for my soul. The time after dinner I spent with Mme. de La Troche at the Arsenal. In the evening I had your letter, which threw me back into my first grief, and tonight I shall finish this at Mme. de Coulanges's, where I shall hear some news. For my part this is all I know about, together with the regrets of all those you have left here. If I felt like it the whole of my letter could be full of people's good wishes.

Paris
Wednesday 18 February 1671

I do urge you, dear heart, to look after your eyes – as to mine, you know they must be used up in your service. You must realize, my love, that because of the way you write to me I have to cry when I read your letters. To understand something of the state I am in over you, add to the tenderness and natural feeling I have for you this little circumstance that I am quite sure you love me, and then consider my overwhelming emotion. Naughty girl! Why do you sometimes hide such precious treasures from me? Are you afraid I might die of joy? But aren't you also afraid that I should die of sorrow at believing I see the opposite?. . . .

Paris
Wednesday 8 April 1671

I am beginning to get your letters on Sundays, a sign that the weather is fine. How good your letters are, my dear! There are passages fit to print; one of these days you will find that one of your friends has pirated you.

You are in a retreat. You have found our poor Sisters and have a cell there. But don't dig too deeply into your mind. Reflections are sometimes so gloomy that they lead to death; you know we have to glide a little over the surface of thoughts. You will find joy in that House of which you are mistress.* I am amazed at the attire of your ladies for communion; it is extraordinary and I could never get used to it. I believe that you will have to lower your own coiffes more. I can understand that you would have far less trouble not curling your hair than keeping quiet about what you see. . . .

Paris
Sunday 26 April 1671

It is Sunday 26th April and this letter will not go until Wednesday, but this is not a letter, it is a story Moreuil has just told me for your benefit about what has happened at Chantilly concerning Vatel. I wrote to you last Wednesday that he had stabbed himself; here is the affair in detail.

The King arrived on Thursday evening. Hunting, lanterns, moonlight, a gentle walk, supper served in a spot carpeted with daffodils – everything was perfect. They had supper. There was no roast at one or two tables because of several unexpected guests. That upset Vatel, and he said more than once, "I am dishonoured; this is a humiliation I will not bear," He said to Gourville, "I don't know where I am, I haven't slept for twelve nights. Help me give orders,"

---

* *Order of the Visitation at Aix. The Order founded by Mère de Chantal, great-grandmother of Mme de Grignan.*

Gourville comforted him as far as he could, but this roast missing, not from the King's table but from the twenty-fifth down, constantly came back to his mind. Gourville told all this to Monsieur le Prince. Monsieur le Prince went to Vatel's room and said to him, "Vatel, everything is all right, nothing was so perfect as the King's supper." But he answered, "Monseigneur, your kindness is overwhelming, but I know that there was no roast at two tables." "Not at all," said Monsieur le Prince, "don't upset yourself, everything is going splendidly." Night falls. The fireworks are a failure owing to fog, and they cost 16,000 francs. By four in the morning Vatel was rushing round everywhere and finding everything wrapped in slumber. He found a small supplier who only had two loads of fish. "Is that all?" he asked. "Yes Sir." He did not know that Vatel had sent round to all the seaports. Vatel waited a short time, the other suppliers did not turn up, he lost his head and thought there would be no more fish. He went and found Gourville and said, "Sir, I shall never survive this disgrace, my honour and my reputation are at stake." Gourville laughed at him. Vatel went to his room, put his sword up against the door and ran it through his heart. But that was only at the third attempt, for the first two were not mortal. Then he fell dead. Meanwhile the fish was coming in from all quarters. They looked for Vatel to allocate it, went to his room, broke in the door and found him lying in his own blood. . . .

Paris
Monday 27 April 1671

I have a very bad opinion of your listlessness. I am one of the spiteful gossips and I think the worst; it is what I feared. But my dear child, if this misfortune is confirmed do look after yourself. Don't shake yourself up in these early days by your journey to Marseilles; let things settle a bit. Think of your delicate state and that it is only by dint of being careful that you have managed to go full term. I am already very worried about the upset the journey to Brittany will cause to our relationship. If you are pregnant you know that my only object will be to do what you want. I shall make your desires my rule and shall leave any other arrangement or consideration a thousand leagues away. . . .

Les Rochers
Sunday 9 August 1671

. . . . But, my dear, who is to deliver the baby if you have it at Grignan?
Will you get help from a distance? Don't forget last time and don't forget what
happened the first time, and how you needed a skilled and quick-acting man.
Sometimes you are worried about how you can prove your affection; here is
just the occasion when I am asking you for a proof. Moreover I shall be so
grateful if for love of me you will take a great deal of care of yourself. Ah, my
dear, how easy it will always be to pay your debt to me! Could treasures and all
the wealth in the world give me as much joy as your affection? But also, if you
reverse the medal, hell is no worse that the opposite. . . .

Paris
Wednesday 6 April 1672

. . . . M. de Grignan is asking for a very good jerkin. This is a matter of
seven or eight hundred francs. What has become of a very fine one he had?
Do let me remind you, my love, that one doesn't exactly give away rags of this
kind and that even the pieces are good. For God's sake do save at least some
of the excessive expense. Without knowing exactly what effect it will have,
do keep a general eye open so as not to let anything be lost and not to relax
your efforts about anything. Don't, as they say, throw away the handle after
the axe. . . .

Paris
Sunday 3 July 1672

. . . . I confess I was quite overcome with sorrow when my manservant
came and told me there were no letters for me in the post. This is the second
time that I have had no word from you. I think it might be the fault of the post
or of your travelling, but it still is very unpleasant. As I am not used to the
pain I suffer on these occasions I am bearing it with rather a bad grace. You
have been so ill that I keep feeling some disaster will befall you, and you have
been so surrounded with disasters since you have no longer been with me that
I have reason to fear them all, just because you don't fear any. Good-bye my
dearest. I would say more had I had news from you. . . .

Paris

Monday 10 January 1689

We often think alike, my dear; I even think I wrote from Les Rochers what you write in your last letter about time. It is true: We consent to its passing. There is nothing so dear or precious in the days left to me now. I used to feel them thus when you were at the Hotel de Carnavalet. I have told you so a score of times, I never came home without appreciable joy; I savoured it, got the best out of the hours, was greedy over them, felt like weeping every evening at their flight. In separation this is no longer so, you don't bother about them, you even hurry them along sometimes. You hope, you hasten towards a time you want or aspire to. In fact you are doing a piece of tapestry you want to finsh, you are generous with the days, you throw them at whoever wants them. But, my dear one, suddenly I confess that when I think where this squandering and impatience with the hours and days is leading me, I tremble and find I cannot rely on any more of them, and reason shows me what I shall probably find in my way. My dear, these thoughts are for myself alone, and I mean to abandon them with you and try to make them really valid for myself. . . .

SARAH, DUCHESS OF MARLBOROUGH
1660–1744

Very few biographical details are known about Sarah Jennings, later to become Sarah Churchill, Duchess of Marlborough and destined to play a significant role in English history. As a young woman she was Maid of Honour to Princess Anne and from that position she acquired a powerful position of ascendancy over her. She died an octogenarian and a millionairess. She had a lack of tact and a violent temper and her relationship with her mother was stormy – as this letter testifies. However, they remained attached to each other so long as they lived apart. This letter was written to her mother soon after her own marriage, probably between 1675 and 1677.

. . . . I have thought very often since I left, dear Mother, what was the reason of all the disorder and ill humour the night and morning before I came away; and if I thought I had done anything that you had reason to take ill I should be very angry with myself, but I am very sure I did not intend anything but give you the duty I ought, and if against my will and knowledge I have committed any fault I hope you will forgive it and I beg you will consider how often I stopped the coach as we came home and begged you to come in which I could do for not other reason but for leave [fear] you should get your death, and what reason had you when you came here to say so many cruel things to me and Betty Moody [Mowdie] which I can't but take to myself. The post is going and I can say no more but that I hope I shall see you or hear from you very soon, and that I will ever be your most dutiful daughter whatever you are to me.

"Churchill"

REQUESTS, COMPLAINTS
AND ADVICE

1672–1760

JOHN STRYPE
1643–1737

John Strype was an ecclesiastical historian and biographer, educated at St Paul's School, Jesus College and Catherine Hall, Cambridge. Amongst other works, he wrote a life of Cranmer and many letters which are to be found in the library of Cambridge University Press.

The following extensive letter was written to his mother from Jesus College Cambridge in 1662 and presents a vivid picture of college life in the seventeenth century.

Good Mother,

Yours of the 24th instant I gladly received, expecting indeed one a Week before, but I understand both by Waterson and yourself of your indisposednesse then to write. The reason you receive this no sooner is, because I had as mind (knowing of this honest woman's setting out so suddenly for London from hence, and her businesse laying so neer to Petticote Lane,) that she should deliver it into your hands, that so you may the better, and more fully heare of me, and know how it fareth with me. She is my laundress; make her welcome, and tell her how you would have my linen washed, as you were saying in your Letter. I am very glad to hear that you and my brother Johnson do agree so well, that I believe you account an unusual courtesie, that he should have you out to the Cake-House. However, pray Mother, be careful of yourself and do not over-walk yourself, for that is wont to bring you upon a sick bed. I hear also my brother Sayer is often a visitor: truly I am glad of it. I hope your Children may be comforts to you now you are growing old. Remember me back again most kindly to my brother Sayer.

Concerning the taking up of my Things, 'tis true I gave one shilling too much in the hundred: but why I gave so much, I thought indeed I had given you an account in that same letter: but it seems I have not. The only reason is, because they were a Scholar's goods: it is common to make them pay one shilling more than the Town's people. Dr Pearson himself payed so, and several other lads in this College: and my Tutor told me they would expect so much of me, being a Scholar: and I found it so.

Do not wonder so much at our Commons: they are more than many Colleges have. Trinity itself (where Herring and Davies are) which is the famousest College in the University, have but three half-pence. We have roast meat, dinner and supper, throughout the weeke; and such meate as you know I not use to care for; and that is Veal: but now I have learnt to eat it. Sometimes, neverthelesse, we have boiled meat, with pottage; and beef and mutton, which I am glad of; except Fridays and Saturdays, and sometimes Wednesdays; which days we have Fish at dinner, and tansy or pudding for supper. Our parts then are slender enough. But there is this remedy; we may retire unto the Butteries, and there take a half-penny loafe and butter or cheese; or else to the Kitchen, and take there what the Cook hath. But, for my part, I am sure, I never visited the Kitchen yet, since I have been here, and the Butteries but seldom after meals; unlesse for a Ciza, that is for a Farthing-worth of Small-Beer: so that lesse than a Peny in Beer doth serve me a whole Day. Nevertheless sometimes we have Exceedings: then we have two or three Dishes (but that is very rare): otherwise never but one: so that a Cake and a Cheese would be very welcome to me: and a Neat's tongue, or some such thing, if it would not require too much money. If you do intend to send me any thing, do not send it yet, until you hear further of me: for I have many things to send for, which may all I hope be put into that Box you have at home: but what they are, I shall give you an account of hereafter, when I would have them sent: and that is, when I have got me a Chamber: for as yet, I am in a Chamber that doth not at all please me. I have thoughts of one, which is a very handsome one, and one pair of stairs high, and that looketh into the Master's garden. The price is but 20s per annum, ten whereof a Knight's son, and lately admitted into this College, doth pay: though he did not come till about Midsummer, so that I shall have but 10s to pay a year: besides my income, which may be about 40s or thereabouts. Mother, I kindly thank you for your Orange pills you sent me. If you are not too straight of money, send me some such thing by the woman, and a pound or two of Almonds and Raisons. But first ask her if she will carry them, or if they be not too much trouble to her. I do much approve of your agreeing with the Carrier quarterly: he was indeed telling me of it, that you had agreed with him for it: and I think he means both yours and mine. Make your bargain sure with him.

I understand by your Letter that you are very inquisitive to know how things stand with me here. I believe you may be well enough satisfied by the Woman. My breakings-out are now all gone. Indeed I was afraid at my first coming it would have proved the Itch: but I am fairly rid on it; but I fear I shall get it, let me do what I can: for there are many here that have it cruelly. Some of them take strong purges that would kill a horse, weeks together for it, to get it away, and yet are hardly rid of it. At my first Coming I laid alone: but since, my Tutor desired me to let a very clear lad lay with me, and an Alderman's son of Colchester, which I could not deny, being newly come: he hath laid with me now for almost a fortnight, and will do till he can provide himself with a Chamber. I have been with all my Acquaintance, who have entreated me very courteously, especially Jonathan Houghton. I went to his Chamber the Friday night I first came, and there he made me stay and sup with him, and would have had me laid with him that night, and was extraordinary kind to me. Since, we have been together pretty often. He excused himselfe, that he did not come to see me before he went; and that he did not write to me since he had been come. He hath now, or is about obtaining, £10 more from the College.

We go twice a day to Chapel; in the morning about 7, and in the Evening about 5. After we come from Chapel in the morning, which is towards 8, we go to the Butteries for our breakfast, which usually is five Farthings; and halfepenny loaf and butter, and a cize of beer. But sometimes I go to an honest House near the College, and have a pint of milk boiled for my breakfast.

Truly I was much troubled to hear that my Letter for Ireland is not yet gone. I wish if Mr. Jones is not yet gone, that might be sent some other way. Indeed I wish I could see my cousin James Bonnell here within three or four years: for I believe our University is less strict to observe lads that do not in every point conforme, than theirs at Dublin; though ours be bad enough. Pray remember me to my Uncle, and all my friends there, when you write. Remember me to my cousin James Knox. I am glad he is recovered from his dangerous sickness, whatsoever it is; for I cannot make any thing of it, as you have written it. And this, for want of Paper, I end, desiring heartily to be remembered to all my Friends. Excuse me to my Brother and Sister that they have not heard from me yet. Next week I hope to write to them both. Excuse my length, I thought I would answer your Letter to the full. I remaine your dutiful Son,

J. STRIJP

These for his honoured Mother
Mrs. Hester Stryp widdow,
dwelling in Petticoat Lane, right over
against the Five Ink-Hornes, without Bishops-Gate,
in London.

ETON SCHOOLBOY

In the seventeenth century, small boys of the privileged classes were beginning to be educated as English gentlemen away from home at public school. Here is a letter, the exact date unknown, to his mother, from a small boy boarding at Eton.

My dear Mama,

I wright to tell you I am very retched, and my chilblains is worse agen. I have not made any progress and I do not think I shall. i am very sorry to be such expense to you, but i do not think this schule is very good. One of the fellows has taken the crown of my new hat for a target, he has burrowed my watch to make wheal, with the works, but it won't act – me and him have tried to put the works back, but we think some wheels are missing as they won't fit. I hope Matilda's cold is better i am glad she is not at a schule. I think i have got the consumption the boys at the place are not gentlemen but of course you did not know that when you sent me hear, i will try not to get bad habits.

The trousers have worn out at the knee, i think the tailor must have cheated you, the buttons have come off, and they are loos at the back i don't think the food is good but I should not mind if I was stronger. The peace of meet i sent you is off the beef we had on Sunday but on other days it is more stringey. There are black beetles in the kitchen and sometimes they cook them in the dinner which can't be wholesome when you are not strong. Dear mama

I hope you and papa are well and dont mind my being uncomfortable because i dont think i shall last long please send me some more money as i owe 8d if you can't spare it i can burrow it of a boy who is going to leave at the half-quarter and then he won't ask for it again but perhaps you wd not like me to be obliged to his parents as they are trades people and I think you deal at their shop i did not mention it or i dare say they would have put it down in the bill.
Your loving but retched son

JOHN BYROM
1692–1763

John Byrom was a minor literary and scientific figure and was made a fellow of the Royal Society in 1724. He invented a new form of short-hand. He also wrote the words to 'Christians Awake! Salute the happy morn'.

JOHN BYROM TO HIS SON EDWARD.

Gray's Inn
Tues. night
May 4, 1736

Dr. Tedy: I had thy letter last post, which I like very well; ay, write again, for by thy writing thou wilt learn to write. The Prince of Wales is married to be sure; I saw him and his lady the other night in a cloud of dust that hindered me from asking them any questions, and as she could not talk English neither, I thought it best not to make her stay in the dust.

And so you have had burnfires and bells and shooting and drinking; for such is the custom of the world upon such occasions.

Pray tell me, Tedy, do you think that if a man by drinking another man's health should lose his own, that other man would get it?

Observe, Tedy, how simple and foolish men make themselves when they drink strong drink, and say to thyself, I will not be like these men, nor put any thing into my body that will take away understanding from my mind.

Yes, I have sold North, I believe, for the gentleman that has him does not speak so much in his favour as you do. The eating his head off means that he would eat as much hay and corn as he is worth, and that they call eating his head off; which is indeed an odd expression, for how can he eat his own head?

he might sooner eat his legs, if he was disposed to feed upon himself, which he hardly will.

In France it is a common saying of a man that has spent his estate, to say that he has eaten his estate up, though the ground be still there; but with respect to him who has then no use of it, it might as well have been eaten away.

As for the price of him I made no bargain, because I sold him to a friend; now friends do not, or should not, differ much about money in such cases. I desire no more than what he be esteemed worth, and my friend desires to give me no less.

Pray my service to Mr. High Sheriff, and thank him; if I must keep the gaol I must have you for the under gaoler, and we will use the poor prisoners very well.

Pray return my service to Ellen Nelson, and when you write let me know how she does, for I reckon her amongst you always.

I thought to have writ to mamma, and my paper is ended, and it is late, so give my dear love to her, and tell her I'll write to her next; and conster this for her, Deus benicat vobis omnibus. Amen

EARL OF CHESTERFIELD
1694–1773

From 1737 Lord Chesterfield, statesman and diplomat, wrote almost daily letters to his illegitimate son, Philip Stanhope (1732–1768). They were not written for publication but were instructions on etiquette and the worldly arts of his day. After their publication in 1774 they became a handbook of good manners.

Despite the fact that Philip has left school, his father certainly doesn't think that his education is finished and he writes with great pomposity, giving his son the benefit of what he believes to be his superior knowledge on the ways of the world.

London
October 9 o.s.1747

Dear Boy:

People of your age have, commonly, an unguarded frankness about them; which makes them the easy prey and bubbles of the artful and the experienced; they look upon every knave or fool, who tells them that he is their friend, to be really so; and pay that profession simulated friendship with an indiscreet and unbounded confidence, always to their loss, often to their ruin. Beware, therefore, now that you are coming into the world, of these proffered friendships. Receive them with great civility, but with great incredulity too; and pay them with compliments, but not with confidence. Do not let your vanity and self-love make you suppose that people become your friends at first sight or even upon a short acquaintance. Real friendship is a slow grower; and never thrives, unless ingrafted upon a stock of known and reciprocal merit. There is another kind of nominal friendship among young people, which is warm for the time, but, by good luck, of short duration. This friendship is hastily produced, by their being accidentally thrown together, and pursuing the same course of riot and debauchery. A fine friendship, truly; and well cemented by drunkenness and lewdness. It should rather be called a conspiracy against morals and good manners, and be punished as such by the civil magistrate. However, they have the impudence and folly to call this confederacy a friendship. They lend one another money, for bad purposes; they engage in quarrels, offensive and defensive, for their accomplices; they tell one another all they know and often more too, when, of a sudden some accident disperses them and they think no more of each other, unless it be to betray and laugh at their imprudent confidence. Remember to make a great difference between companions and friends; for a very complaisant and agreeable companion may, and often does, prove a very improper and a very dangerous friend. People will, in a great degree, and not without reason, form their opinion of you, upon that which they have of your friends; and there is a Spanish proverb, which says very justly, *Tell me whom you live with, and I will tell you who you are.* One may fairly suppose, that a man, who makes a knave or a fool his friend, has something very bad to do or conceal. But, at the same time that you carefully decline the friendship of knaves and fools, if it can be called friendship, there is no occasion to make either of them your enemies, wantonly, and unprovoked; for they are numerous bodies: and I would rather choose a secure neutrality, than alliance, or war, with either of them. You may be a declared enemy to their vices and follies, without being marked out by them as a personal one. Their enmity is the next dangerous thing to their friendship. Have a real reserve with almost everybody; and have a seeming reserve with almost nobody; for it is very disagreeable to seem reserved, and very dangerous not to be so. Few people find the true medium; many are ridiculously mysterious and reserved upon trifles; and many imprudently communicative of all they know. . . .

Adieu.

London
December 30 o.s. 1748

Dear Boy

. . . . Your dress (as insignificant a thing as dress is in itself) is now become an object worthy of some attention; for, I confess, I cannot help forming some opinion of a man's sense and character from his dress; and I believe, most people do as well as myself. Any affectation whatsoever in dress implies, in my mind, a flaw in the understanding. Most of our young fellows here display some character or other by their dress; some affect the tremendous, and wear a great and fiercely cocked hat, an enormous sword, a short waist-coat and a black cravat; these I should be almost tempted to swear the peace against, in my own defence, if I were not convinced that they are but meek asses in lion's skins. Others go in brown frocks, leather breeches, great oaken cudgels in their hands, their hats uncocked, and their hair unpowdered; and imitate grooms, stage-coachmen, and country bumpkins so well, in their outsides, that I do not make the least doubt of their resembling them equally in their insides. A man of sense carefully avoids any particular character in his dress; he is accurately clean for his own sake; but all the rest is for other people's. He dresses as well, and in the same manner, as the people of sense and fashion of the place where he is. If he dresses better, as he thinks, that is, more than they, he is a fop; if he dresses worse, he is unpardonably negligent: but, of the two, I would rather have a young fellow too much than too little dressed; the excess on that side will wear off, with a little age and reflection; but if he is negligent at twenty, he will be a sloven at forty, and stink at fifty years old. Dress yourself fine, where others are fine; and plain where others are plain; but take care always that your clothes are well made, and fit you, for otherwise they will give you a very awkward air. When you are once well dressed for the day think no more of it afterwards; and without any stiffness for fear of discomposing that dress, let all your motions be as easy and natural as if you had no clothes on at all. So much for dress, which I maintain to be a thing of consequence in the polite world.

As to manners, good-breeding, and the Graces, I have so often entertained you upon these important subjects, that I can add nothing to what I have formerly said. . . .

Adieu!

London
August 10 o.s. 1749

Dear Boy

. . . . There is a certain dignity of manners absolutely necessary, to make even the most valuable character either respected or respectable.

Horse-play, romping, frequent and loud fits of laughter, jokes, waggery, and indiscriminate familiarity, will sink both merit and knowledge into a degree of contempt. They compose at most a merry fellow; and a merry fellow was never yet a respectable man. Indiscriminate familiarity either offends your superiors, or else dubs you their dependent, and led captain. It gives your inferiors just, but troublesome and improper claims of equality. A joker is near akin to a buffoon; and neither of them is the least related to wit. Whoever is admitted or sought for, in company, upon any other account than that of his merit and manners, is never respected there, but only made use of. We will have such-a-one, for he sings prettily; we will invite such-a-one to a ball, for he dances well; we will have such-a-one at supper, for he is always joking and laughing; we will ask another, because he plays deep at all games, or because he can drink a great deal. These are all vilifying distinctions, mortifying preferences, and exclude all ideas of esteem and regard. Whoever is *had* (as it is called) in company for the sake of any one thing singly, is singly that thing, and will never be considered in any other light; consequently never respected, let his merits be what they will.

This dignity of manners, which I recommend so much to you, is not only different from pride, as true courage is from blustering, or true wit from joking; but is absolutely inconsistent with it; for nothing vilifies and degrades more than pride. The pretensions of the proud man are oftener treated with sneers and contempt than with indignation; as we offer ridiculously too little to a tradesman who asks ridiculously too much for his goods; but we do not haggle with one who only asks a just and reasonable price.

Abject flattery and indiscriminate assentation degrade as much as indiscriminate contradiction and noisy debate disgust. But a modest assertion of one's own opinion, and a complaisant acquiescence in other people's, preserve dignity.

Vulgar, low expressions, awkward motions and address, vilify, as they imply, either a very low turn of mind, or low education and low company.

Frivolous curiosity about trifles, and a laborious attention to little objects, which neither require nor deserve a moment's thought, lower a man; who from thence is thought (and not unjustly) incapable of greater manners. Cardinal de Retz, very sagaciously, marked out Cardinal Chigi for a little mind, from the moment he told him he had wrote three years the same pen, and that it was an excellent good one still.

A certain degree of exterior seriousness in looks and motions gives dignity, without excluding wit and decent cheerfulness, which are always serious themselves. A constant smirk upon the face, and a whiffling activity of the body, are strong indications of futility. Whoever is in a hurry, shows that the thing he is about is too big for him. Haste and hurry are very different things. . . .

Adieu!

London
September 22 o.s. 1749

Dear Boy

. . . . He told me then, that in company you were frequently most *provokingly* inattentive, absent, and *distrait*. That you came into a room and presented yourself, very awkwardly: that at table you constantly threw down knives, forks, napkins, bread, etc., and that you neglected your person and dress, to a degree unpardonable at any age, and much more so at yours.

These things, how immaterial soever they may seem to people who do not know the nature of mankind, give me who know them to be exceedingly material, very great concern. I have long distrusted you, and therefore frequently admonished you, upon these articles; and I tell you plainly, that I shall not be easy till I hear a very different account of them. I know no one thing more offensive to a company, than that inattention and *distraction*. It is showing them the utmost contempt; and people never forgive contempt. No man is *distrait* with the man he fears, or the woman he loves; which is a proof that every man can get the better of that *distraction*, when he thinks it worth his while to do so; and take my word for it, it is always worth his while. For my own part I would rather be in company with a dead man , than with an absent one; for if the dead man gives me no pleasure, at least he shows me no contempt; whereas the absent man, silently indeed, but very plainly, tells me that he does not think me worth his attention. . . .

In short, I give you fair warning, that when we meet, if you are absent in mind, I will be absent in body; for it will be impossible for me to stay in the same room; and if at table you throw down your knife, plate, bread, etc., and hack the wing of a chicken for half an hour, without being able to cut it off, and your sleeve all the time in another dish, I must rise from the table to escape the fever you would certainly give me. Good God! how I should be shocked, if you came into my room, for the first time, with two left legs, presenting yourself with all the graces and dignity of a tailor, and your clothes hanging upon you, like those in Monmouth Street, upon tenter-hooks! whereas I expect, nay require, to see you present yourself with the easy and genteel air of a man of fashion, who has kept good company. I expect you not only well dressed but very well dressed; I expect a gracefulness in all your motions, and something particularly engaging in your address. All this I expect, and all this it is your power, by care and attention, to make me find; but to tell you the plain truth, if I do not find it, we shall not converse very much together; for I cannot stand inattention and awkwardness; it would endanger my health. . . .

When I was of your age, I desired to shine, as far as I was able, in every part of life; and was as attentive to my manners, my dress, and my air, in company on evenings, as my books and my tutor in the mornings. . . .

This letter is very long, and possibly a very tedious one; but my anxiety for your perfection is so great, and particularly at this critical and decisive period of your life, that I am only afraid of omitting, but never of repeating, or dwelling too long upon anything that I think may be of the least use to you. Have the same anxiety for yourself, that I have for you, and all will do well. Adieu, my dear child.

EDWARD GIBBON
1737-1793

Edward Gibbon had a privileged up-bringing but was a feeble and sickly child. He states in his memoirs that "the death of a new-born child before that of its parents may seem an unnatural, but it is strictly a probable, event: since of any given number the greater part are extinguished before their ninth year, before they possess the faculties of the mind or body. . . . So feeble was my constitution, so precarious my life, that, in the baptism of each of my brothers, my father's prudence successively repeated my Christian name of Edward, that, in case of the departure of the eldest son, this patronymic appellation might be still perpetuated in the family." However, his five brothers and one sister all died in infancy and so he was the one to carry the family name.

After a university education his father became a Member of Parliament, representing Petersfield for the Tories. He sent his son to Westminster School from where the boy went on to attend Magdalen College, Oxford studying Classics and by his own admission, wasting time. After a brief flirtation with Catholicism and a five year exile in Lausanne, Gibbon served in the Hampshire militia and then as a Member of Parliament. He is the author of *The History of the Decline and Fall of the Roman Empire* which was issued in six volumes and published in 1776 and 1788. The Duke of Gloucester on accepting a volume remarked affably, "Another damned thick, square book! Always scribble, scribble, scribble! Eh, Mr Gibbon?"

In the following letter to his father Edward is requesting that he should have his father's approval and allowance to go to Lausanne to study.

1760

Dear Sir,

An address in writing, from a person who has the pleasure of being with you every day, may appear singular. However, I have preferred this method, as upon paper I can speak without a blush, and be heard without interruption. If my letter displeases you, impute it, dear Sir, only to yourself. You have treated me, not like a son, but like a friend. Can you be surprised that I should communicate to a friend, all my thoughts, and all my desires? Unless the friend approve them, let the father never know them; or at least, let him know at the same time, that however reasonable, however eligible, my scheme may appear to me, I would rather forget it for ever, than cause him the slightest uneasiness.

When I first returned to England, attentive to my future interest, you were so good as to give me hopes of a seat in parliament. This seat, it was supposed would be an expence of fifteen hundred pounds. This design flattered my vanity, as it might enable me to shine in so august an assembly. It flattered a nobler passion; I promised myself that by the means of this seat I might be one day the instrument of some good to my country. But I soon perceived how little a mere virtuous inclination, unassisted by talents, could contribute towards that great end; and a very short examination discovered to me, that those talents had not fallen to my lot. Do not, dear Sir, impute this ever else I may be ignorant of, I think I know myself, and shall always without repugnance. I shall say nothing of the most intimate acquaintance with his country and language, so absolutely necessary to every senator. Since they may be acquired, to alledge my deficiency in them, would seem only the plea of laziness. But I shall say with great truth, that I never possessed that gift of speech, the first requisite of an orator, which use and labour may improve, but which nature alone can neither acquire popularity, bear up against opposition, nor mix with ease in the crowds of public life. That even my genius (if you will allow me any) is better qualified for the deliberate compositions of the expected. Objection would disconcert me; and as I am incapable of explaining to others, what I do not thoroughly understand myself, I should be meditating, while I ought to be answering. I even want necessary prejudices of party, and of nation. In popular assemblies, it is often necessary to inspire them; and never orator inspired well a passion, which he did not feel himself. Suppose me even mistaken in my own character; to set out with the repugnance such an opinion must produce, offers but an indifferent prospect. But I hear you say, it is not necessary that every man should enter into parliament with such exalted hopes. It is to acquire a title the most glorious of any in a free country, and to employ the weight and consideration it gives, in the service of one's friends. Such motives, though not glorious, yet are not dishonourable; and if we had a borough in our command, if you could bring me in without any great expence, or if our fortune enabled us to despise that expence, then indeed I should think them of the greatest strength. But with our private fortune, is it worth while to purchase at so high a rate, a title, honourable in itself, but which I must share with every fellow that can lay out fifteen hundred pounds? Besides, dear Sir, a merchandise is of a little value to the owner, when he is resolved not to sell it.

I should affront your penetration, did I not suppose you now see the drift of this letter. It is to appropriate to another use the sum with which you destined to bring me into parliament; to employ it, not in making me great, but in rendering me happy. I have often heard you say yourself, that the allowance you had been so indulgent as to grant me, though very liberal in regard to your estate, was yet but small when compared with the almost necessary extravagancies of the age. I have indeed found it so, notwithstanding a good deal of economy, and an exemption from many of the common expences of youth. This, dear Sir, would be a way of supplying these deficiencies, without any additional expence to you.– But I forebear.– If you think my proposals reasonable, you want no entreaties to engage you to comply with them; if otherwise, all will be without effect.

All that I am afraid of, dear Sir, is, that I should seem not so much asking a favour, as this really is, as exacting a debt. After all I can say, you will still remain the best judge of my good, and your own circumstances. Perhaps, like most landed gentlemen, an addition to my annuity would suit you better, than a sum of money given at once; perhaps the sum itself may be too considerable. Whatever you shall think proper to bestow upon me, or in whatever manner, will be received with equal gratitude.

I intended to stop here; but as I abhor the least appearance of art I think it will be better to lay open my whole scheme at once. The unhappy war which now desolates Europe, will oblige me to defer seeing France till a peace. But that reason can have no influence upon Italy, a country which every scholar must long to see; should you grant my request, and not disapprove of my manner of employing your bounty, I would leave England this Autumn, and pass the Winter at Lausanne, with M. de Voltaire and my old friends. The armies no longer obstruct my passage, and it must be indifferent to you, whether I am at Lausanne or at London during their Winter, since I shall not be at Beriton. In the spring I would cross the Alps, and after some stay in Italy, as the war must then be terminated, return home through France; to live happily with you and my dear mother. I am now two-and-twenty; a tour must take up a considerable time, and though I believe you have no thoughts of settling me soon, (and I am sure I have not,) yet so many things may intervene, that the man who does not travel early, runs a great risk of not travelling at all. But this part of my scheme, as well as the whole, I submit entirely to you.

Permit me, dear Sir, to add, that I do not know whether the complete compliance with my wishes could increase my love and gratitude; but that I am very sure, no refusal could diminish those sentiments with which I shall always remain, dear Sir,

Your most dutiful and obedient son and servant,

E. Gibbon, junior.

AUSTRIAN AND
PRUSSIAN COMPOSERS
AND WRITERS

1769–1786

WOLFGANG AMADEUS MOZART
1756–1791

Wolfgang Amadeus Mozart was born in Salzburg on 27th January 1756. He was the son of Leopold, then aged 37, and Marianne. His was a musical family. His father was a violinist and a minor composer and court musician at Salzburg and his elder sister, Maria Anna or Nannerl as she was called, had a fine singing voice and was an excellent keyboard player. By the time Mozart was 7 he was composing as well as showing great talent as a violinist and clavier player. From 1762 the family made a series of concert tours across Europe. Mozart's exceptional talent ensured that even at this early age he was internationally known.

The tours must have been physically exhausting and Mozart was not of the strongest constitution. It has been suggested that his father pushed him too hard at an early age, probably because the family had need of the money. However, he not only survived but was enriched by the musical experiences of Europe, meeting many famous composers and performers and forming a very definite critical faculty which is illustrated in many of his letters. His relationship with his father, though sometimes strained, remained close and loving.

In 1782 he married Constanze Weber. Theirs was a happy marriage and they had six children, though only two survived. He died of uraemia in 1791, neglected by all but a few friends and his devoted wife. He was badly in debt and was buried in a pauper's grave.

Mozart was a prolific letter writer and his correspondence reveals an exuberant and often argumentative but highly intelligent man of firm opinions and great tenderness. His account of his mother's illness and death is detailed and harrowing (she was with Mozart in Paris) and after she had gone he remained in close touch with his father and sister. Most of the letters included here are domestic in tone but he also wrote at length to his father about their shared passion of music.

MOZART TO HIS MOTHER

Worgl
13 December 1769

Dearest Mamma,

My heart is completely enchanted with all these pleasures, because it is so jolly on this journey, because it is so warm in the carriage and because our coachman is a fine fellow who, when the road gives him the slightest chance, drives so fast. Papa will have already described the journey to Mamma. The reason why I am writing to Mamma is to show her that I know my duty and that I am with the deepest respect her devoted son

Wolfgang Mozart

Milan
20 October 1770

My dear Mamma,

I cannot write much, for my fingers are aching from composing so many recitatives. Mamma, I beg you to pray for me, that my opera may go well and that we may be happy together again. . . .

MOZART TO HIS FATHER

Paris
9 July 1778

Monsieur mon très cher Père

I hope that you are now prepared to hear with fortitude one of the saddest and most painful stories; indeed my last letter of the 3rd will have told you that no good news could be hoped for. On that very same day, the 3rd, at twenty-one minutes past ten at night my mother fell asleep peacefully in the Lord; indeed, when I wrote to you, she was already enjoying the blessings of Heaven – for all then was over. I wrote to you during that night and I hope that you and my dear sister will forgive me for this slight but very necessary deception, for as I judged from my own grief and sorrow what yours would be, I could not indeed bring myself suddenly to shock you with this dreadful news!

But I hope that you have now summoned up courage to hear the worst, and that after you have at first given way to natural, and only too well justified tears and anguish, will eventually resign yourself to the will of God and worship His unsearchable, unfathomable and all-wise providence.

My dearest father! Do not give way! Dearest sister! Be firm! You do not as yet know your brother's good heart – for he has not yet been able to prove it. My two beloved ones! Take care of your health! Remember that you have a son, a brother, who is doing his utmost to make you happy . . . .

The following letter is included as much for its revelation into medical treatments of the day as for Mozart's care and diligence in looking after his mother.

Paris
31 July 1778

Monsieur mon très cher Père!

From time to time I have fits of melancholy – but I find that the best way to get rid of them is to write or receive letters, which invariably cheer me up again. . . .

First of all, I must tell you that my dear departed mother had to die. No doctor in the world could have saved her this time – for it was clearly the will of God; her time had come – and God wanted to take her to Himself. You think she put off being bled until it was too late? That may be. She did postpone it a little. But I rather agree with the people here who tried to dissuade her from being bled – and to persuade her to take a *lavement*. She would not, however, have this – and I did not venture to say anything, as I do not understand these things and consequently should have been to blame if it had not suited her. If it had been by own case I would have consented at once – for this treatment is very popular here – whoever has an inflammation takes a *lavement* – and the cause of my mother's illness was nothing but an internal inflammation – or at least was diagnosed as such. I cannot tell you accurately how much blood she was let, for it is measured here not by the ounce but by the plate; they took a little less than two platefuls. The surgeon said that it was very necessary – but it was so terribly hot that day that he did not dare to bleed her any more. For a few days she was all right. Then diarrhoea started –

but no one paid much attention to it, as foreigners who drink a good deal of water commonly find it a laxative. And that is true. I had it myself when I first came to Paris, but since I have given up drinking plain water and always add a little wine, I have been free of this trouble, though indeed, as I cannot altogether do without drinking plain water, I purify it with ice and drink it *en glace* – and take two tumblerfuls before going to bed. Well to continue. On the 19th she complained of headaches, and for the first time she had to spend the day in bed; she was up for the last time on the 18th. On the 20th she complained of shivers – and then fever – so that I gave her an antispasmodic powder. All this time I was very anxious to send for a doctor, but she would not consent; and when I urged her very strongly, she said she had no confidence in a French physician. So I looked about for a German – but as of course I could not go out and leave her, I waited anxiously for M. Heina, who was in the habit of coming regularly every day to see us – but, needless to say, on this occasion he had to stay away for two days! At last he came, but as the doctor was prevented from coming the following day, we could not consult him. Thus he did not come until the 24th. On the previous day, when I had wanted him so badly, I had a great fright – for all of a sudden she lost her hearing. The doctor (an old German of about seventy) gave her a rhubarb powder in wine. I cannot understand that, for people usually say that wine is heating. But when I said so, they all exclaimed; 'How on earth can you say so? Wine is not heating, but strengthening – water is heating' – and meanwhile the poor patient was longing for a drink of fresh water. How gladly would I have given it to her! Most beloved father, you cannot imagine what I endured. But there was no help for it, by Heaven, I had to leave her in the hands of the doctor. All I could do with a good conscience was to pray to God without ceasing that he would order all things for her good. I went about as if I was bereft of my reason. I had ample leisure then for composing, but could not have written a single note. On the 25th the doctor did not come. On the 26th he visited her again. Imagine my feelings when he said to me quite unexpectedly: 'I fear she will not last out the night. If she is taken with pains and has to go to the night-stool, she may die at any moment. You had better see that she makes her confession.' So I ran out to the end of the Chaussée d'Antin, well beyond the Barrière, to find Heina, who I knew was at a concert at the house of a certain Count. He told me he would bring a German priest next day. On my way back, as I was passing, I went in for a moment to see Grimm and Mme.

D'Épinay. They were distressed that I had not told them sooner, for they would have sent their own doctor at once. I had not said anything to them before, because my mother would not have a French doctor – but now I was at my wit's end. They said therefore that they would send their doctor that very evening. When I got home I told my mother that I had met Herr Heina with a German priest who had heard a great deal about me and was longing to hear me play, and that he was coming on the morrow to pay me a visit. She was quite satisfied, and as I thought that she seemed better (although I am no doctor), I said nothing more. . . .

> On 12 March 1781 Mozart went to Vienna at the command of the Archbishop and he frequently wrote to his father complaining of his patron's failure to pay fees for his services. Whilst there he moved into Madame Weber's house as a lodger. She and her daughters were old family friends, but Leopold, Mozart's father, was not happy about the situation and begged Mozart to return to Salzburg. However, Mozart remained, and from his letters home it was obvious that his life at this time was volatile both in work and pleasure. In December he wrote to his father announcing his love for the middle one of the Weber daughters, Constanze.

15 December 1781

. . . . The youngest is still too young to be anything at all. The middle one, however, my dear, kind Constanze, is the martyr among them, and perhaps for that reason the most warm-hearted, the cleverest, and in short the best of them all. She is not ugly, but she is far from beautiful. Her only beauties are a pair of little black eyes and a lovely figure. She is not inclined to extravagance, understands housekeeping, has the kindest heart in the world – I love her, she loves me with all her heart. Tell me, could I wish myself a better wife?. . . .

Vienna
27 July 1781

. . . . Dearest, most beloved father, I implore you by all you hold dear in the world to give your consent to my marriage with my Constanze. Do not suppose that it is just for the sake of getting married. If that were the only reason, I would gladly wait. But I realize that it is absolutely necessary for my

own honour and for that of my girl, and for the sake of my health and spirits.–
. . . .We intend to live very modestly and quietly and yet we shall be happy . . . .

In one of his last letters to his father Mozart discusses at some length
the merits of a visiting oboist from Holland. He ends the letter by
expressing his concern that his father is not well.

Vienna
4 April 1787
. . . . This very moment I have received a piece of news which greatly dis-
tresses me, the more so as I gathered from your last letter that, thank God, you
were very well indeed. But now I hear that you are really ill. I need hardly tell
you how greatly I am longing to receive some reassuring news from yourself.
And I still expect it; although I have now made a habit of being prepared in all
affairs of life for the worst. As death, when we come to consider it closely, is
the true goal of our existence, I have formed during the last few years such
close relations with this best truest friend of mankind, that his image is not
only no longer terrifying to me, but is indeed very soothing and consoling! . . .
. I hope and trust that while I am writing this, you are feeling better. But if,
contrary to all expectation, you are not recovering, I implore you . . . . not to
hide it from me, but to tell me the whole truth or get someone to write it to
me, so that as quickly as is humanly possible I may come to your arms. I
entreat you by all that is sacred – to both of us. Nevertheless I trust that I shall
soon have a reassuring letter from you; and cherishing this pleasant hope, I
and my wife and our little Karl kiss your hands a thousand times and I am ever
your most obedient son
W. A. Mozart

On 29th May 1787 Mozart wrote to Baron Gottfried Von Jacquin, a
friend and pupil,

. . . . I inform you that on returning home to-day I received the sad news of
my most beloved father's death. You can imagine the state I am in.

JOHANN WOLFGANG VON GOETHE
1749–1832

Goethe, the presiding genius of German literature, spent most of his life in Weimar, occupying positions of increasing importance in the government until 1786. He then visited Italy, which had a profound influence on his writing and thinking. In 1791 he was appointed director of the Weimar Court Theatre. His mother, Elisabetha, was embarrassingly besotted with her son. A high-born woman of little brain, she wrote lengthy and ungrammatical letters to him when he was away.

Frankfurt
November 17th, 1786

Dear Son,

An apparition from the underworld could not have amazed me any more than your letter from Rome did! I felt so full of jubilation to see that your desire from earliest youth has now been fulfilled! A journey like this must bring joy and happiness for the rest of life to a person like you, with all your knowledge and with an eagle's clear and wide eye for all things good, grand and beautiful – and not only to you alone but to all who are lucky enough to be living within your sphere of influence. How I would have liked to watch you when you first glanced at St Peters!!! But as you promise to visit me on your return journey, you will then have to tell me all about that in minutest detail. . . . The latest about your old friends is that Pap la Roche is no longer in Speyer, but has bought himself a house in Offenbach, where he intends to live the rest of his life. As for the rest of them, they are still all as they used to be,– none of them has made gigantic progress like you have. But then we have always just been of a lower order, as the late Max Moors once commented. When you come here, all of them will have to be invited and given a real treat: venison and fowl in plenty – it should be really pompous.

Dear Son! A small doubt just came into my mind, as to whether this letter might not get to you properly. I do not know where in Rome you are staying – you are half incognito as you put it – but let us hope for the best.

You will let me know before you come, otherwise I will believe that each coach might bring me my only beloved one,– and disappointed hope is just not for me.

Fare thee well, my favourite, and do think more often of your faithful mother.

Elisabetha Goethe

GEORGIAN ENGLAND

1770–1789

GEORGE III (1738–1820),
QUEEN CHARLOTTE (1744-1818)
AND GEORGE, PRINCE OF WALES (1762–1830)

George III, the eldest son of Frederick, Prince of Wales and Augusta of Saxe-Gotha, came to the throne on the death of his grandfather George II in 1760, his father having died in 1751. George III was a deeply religious man and was determined to clean up the morals of the court. Marriage to Charlotte of Mecklenberg-Strelitz brought him domestic happiness and fifteen children, six daughters and nine sons. Popular outside London, with his kindliness and interest in farming and craftsmanship, "Farmer George" as he was called, was less popular in London and in society with his hostility to the powerful Whig clique. George III suffered from periodic bouts of insanity, almost certainly due to acute intermittent porphyria which was an inherited disease. During a severe attack in the autumn of 1788 Fanny Burney was distressed by his hyperactivity : "The King is so rapid in his meals, that whoever attend him must be rapid also or follow starving." The final and most severe attack began in 1810 and by 1811 he was unable to continue as King. He played no further role in government and the Prince of Wales became Regent.

George, Prince of Wales, the eldest son of George III, was brought up plainly and strictly at Kew but as soon as he could he rejected his parents' life-style and stern advice. He was soon and habitually on bad terms with the King for a number of reasons – his spending, his friends and particularly his liaison with Mrs Fitzherbert. He accumulated huge debts as a result of his association with the Whig opposition to the King, led by Charles James Fox, Edmund Burke and Richard Brinsley Sheridan. In 1795 the Prince married his cousin Caroline of Brunswick, on condition that his debts, some £700,000, were paid. The marriage was a disaster and the couple agreed to lead separate lives even before their only child, Princess Charlotte, was born in 1796.

Despite his extravagancies the Prince was a notable patron of the arts and the Regency was an era of achievement and great personalities, including the writers Shelley, Wordsworth, Scott, Coleridge, Jane Austen; the artists Turner and Constable and the inventors Davey, Farady and Macadam.

The Prince of Wales wrote this letter to the Queen when he was 8 years old. It is his first letter to be preserved. It is undated but probably written around 1770 and is in a very childish hand.

My dear Mama, nothing could have made me so happy as your Majesty's letter, and I will always endeavour to follow the good advice you give me in it being your Majesty's most dutiful son, George P.

Queen Charlotte writes to him the same year:

12 Aug. 1770

My dear son, the demand of a pocket book furnisheth me with an opportunity of stating to you my wishes concerning your future conduct in life. Time draws near when you will be put into the hands of governors, under whose care you will study more manly learning than what you have done hitherto. My advice will be short but sincere, & therefore I flatter myself, not less serviceable to you. Above all things I recommend unto you to fear God, a duty which must lead to all the rest with ease; as His assistance being properly implored will be your guide through every action of life. Abhor all vice, in private as well as in publick, and look upon yourself as obliged to set good examples. Disdain all flattery; it will corrupt your manners and render you contemptible before the world. Do justice unto everybody and avoid partiality. The first will acquire to you happiness in this world as well as hereafter: the latter will make you unhappy, because it leaves after it an unhappy conscience – a situation which seems to me the most wretched in life, as it deprives us of the greatest enjoyment of life, that is, peace of mind. Love and esteem those that are about you. Confide in and act with sincerity towards them, as that alone will be productive of a lasting friendship. Treat nobody with contempt, for that will deprive you of it. Be charitable to everybody, not forgetting your meaner servants. Don't use them with indifference, rather pity them that are obliged to serve, and do unto them as you would be done by. I mean by that you should not think yourself above doing good unto them. The contrary will make you appear vain, and vanity is the root of all vice and a sure proof of ignorance. For what is man to man? We are all equal and become only of consequence by setting good examples to others, and these must be given with a view of doing our duty but not with the idea of superiority, for then the action loses its merits.

Lastly I recommend unto you the highest love, affection and duty towards the King. Look upon him as a friend, nay, as the greatest, the best, and the most deserving of all friends you can possibly find. Try to imitate his virtues, and look upon everything that is in opposition to that duty as destructive to yourself. After this I am sure you can't be unacquainted with what belongs to me as I am the next to the King. Keep in love and friendship with your brothers and sisters, for I am sure they will deserve and require it of you: and as you ought to seek your happiness in that of others, I am sure you will contribute to that of your own family. I, for my part, can safely say, you will contribute greatly towards mine, in following the advice of your most affectionate mother.

> His father, the King, writes to the 18 year old Prince of Wales in a vein not dissimilar to the letters of Lord Chesterfield to his son.

Windsor Castle

14 Aug. 1780

No one feels with more pleasure than I do your nearer approach to manhood, but the parent's joy must be mixed with the anxiety that this period may not be ill spent, as the hour is now come when whatever foundation has been laid must be by application brought to maturity, or every past labour of your instructors will prove abortive.

This has made me think it my duty to state on paper what I trust the goodness of your heart and no want of penetration will make you thoroughly weigh; the contents of this are known to the Queen, whose conduct as a wife as well as mother even malevolence has not dared to mention but in the most respectable terms . . . .

As the eldest of my children, and the one on whom, whenever it shall please Divine Providence to put a period to my existence in this world, the prosperity of my dominions as well as of the rest of my progeny must greatly depend, it is natural that I should be most excessively anxious for your becoming worthy of the station you, according to all human foresight, must fill. Your own good sense must make you feel that you have not made that progress in your studies which, from the ability and assiduity of those placed for that purpose about you, I might have had reason to expect; whilst you have been out of the sight of the world that has been kept under a veil by all those who have surrounded you, nay your foibles have less been perceived than I could have expected; yet your love of dissipation has for some months been with enough ill nature trumpeted in the public papers, and there are those ready to wound me in the severe place by ripping up every error they may be able to find in you. . . .

I certainly shall think it right to make some new arrangement concerning you, but as it is a matter involved with difficulties, I trust you will rest contented when I say that I mean to do it with no greater delay than what must naturally arise from them. Believe me, I wish to make you happy, but the father must, with that object in view, not forget that it is his duty to guide his child to the best of his ability through the rocks that cannot but naturally arise in the outset of youth, and the misfortune is that in other countries national pride makes the inhabitants wish to paint their Princes in the most favourable light, and consequently be silent on any indiscretion; but here most persons, if not concerned in laying ungrounded blame, are ready to trumpet any speck they can find out.

THE PRINCE OF WALES'S REPLY

Windsor Castle,
15 Aug. 1780

I had not the honour of receiving your Majesty's most gracious and affectionate letter till late last night, or else should certainly have answered it before this evening. Permit me to express how extremely sensible I am of the parental attachment & kindness you profess towards me, and allow me to assure you it will be my principal object thro' life to merit them, & to convince you how truly I remain, Sir, (etc.)

FANNY BURNEY
1752–1840

Fanny Burney was described by Dr Johnson as "the sauciest rogue in town". She was chased by George III through the gardens at Kew. She was born in 1752 and died in 1840 aged 87. She led an extraordinary life which took her from the Streatham soirees of Mrs Thrale to the bloodshed of Waterloo via the bedchamber of Queen Charlotte (she was appointed second keeper of the robes to Queen Charlotte in 1786). In 1793 she married General d'Arblay, a French *emigré* in England. She had one child, a son, Alexander.

Similar to Madame de Sévigné in the previous century in France, she knew everyone who was anyone in the late 18th century, including Dr Johnson, Burke and Garrick. Her novels include *Evelina*, *Cecilia* and *Camilla* but it is her diaries and letters for which she is remembered. Her letters to her father, Dr Burney, are like her diaries, full of gossip and detailed reports from court. She was an ardent royalist, hence her father's nickname,"Fanny Bull". Fanny Burney was an amazing woman of the 18th century who, amongst other things, was interned by Napoleon and suffered a mastectomy performed by Napoleon's surgeon without anaesthetic.

FANNY BURNEY TO HER FATHER

Gloucester House
Weymouth
13 July 1789

My dearest Padre's kind letter was most truly welcome to me. When I am so distant, the term of absence or of silence seems long to me.

The bay here is most beautiful; the sea never rough, generally calm and gentle, and the sands perfectly smooth and pleasant. I have not yet bathed, for I have had a cold in my head, which I caught at Lyndhurst, and which makes me fear beginning; but I have hopes to be well enough to-morrow, and thenceforward to ail nothing more. It is my intention to cast away all superfluous complaints into the main ocean, which I think quite sufficiently capacious to hold them; and really my little frame will find enough to carry and manage without them.

Colonel Goldsworthy has just sent me a newspaper containing intelligence that Angelica Kauffmann is making drawings from *Evelina*, for the Empress of Russia! Do you think the Empress of Russia hears of anything now besides Turkey and the Emperor? And is not Angelica Kauffmann dead? Oh what an *Oracle*! for such is the paper called.

His Majesty is in delightful health, and much improved spirits. All agree he never looked better. The loyalty of all this place is excessive; they have dressed out every street with labels of "God save the King": all the shops have it over the doors; all the children wear it in their caps, all the labourers in their hats, and all the sailors in *their voices*, for they never approach the house without shouting it aloud, nor see the King, or his shadow, without beginning to huzza, and going on to three cheers.

The bathing-machines make it their motto over all their windows; and those bathers that belong to the royal dippers wear it in their bandeaus or on their bonnets, to go into the sea; and have it again, in large letters, round their waists, to encounter the waves. Flannel dresses, tucked up, and no shoes nor stockings, with bandeaus and girdles, have a most singular appearance; and when first I surveyed these loyal nymphs it was with some difficulty I kept my features in order. Nor is this all. Think but of the surprise of His Majesty when, the first time of his bathing, he had no sooner popped his royal head under water than a band of music, concealed in a neighbouring machine, struck up "God save great George our King".

One thing, however, was a little unlucky; – when the Mayor and burgesses came with the address, they requested leave to kiss hands; this was graciously accorded; but the Mayor advancing, in a common way, *to take the Queen's hand*, as he might that of any lady mayoress, Colonel Gwynn, who stood by, whispered, "You must kneel, sir." He found, however, that he took no notice of this hint, but kissed the Queen's hand erect. As she passed him, in his way back, the Colonel said, "You should have knelt, sir!"

"Sir," answered the poor Mayor, "I cannot."

"Everybody does, sir."

"Sir, – I have a wooden leg!"

Poor man! 'twas such a surprise! and such an excuse as no one could dispute. But the absurdity of the matter followed; – all the rest did the same; taking the same privilege, by the example, without the same or any cause!

Norbury Park, 23 January 1793

My Dearest Padre – I have been wholly without spirit for writing, reading, working, or even walking or conversing, ever since the first day of my arrival. The dreadful tragedy acted in France has entirely absorbed me. Except the period of the illness of our own inestimable King, I have never been so overcome with grief and dismay, for any but personal and family calamities. Oh what a tragedy! how implacable its villany, and how severe its sorrows! You know my dearest father, how little I had believed such a catastrophe possible: with all the guilt and all the daring already shown, I had still thought this a height of enormity impracticable. And, indeed, without military law throughout the wretched city, it had still not been perpetrated. Good Heaven! – what must have been the sufferings of the few unhardened in crimes who inhabit that city of horrors! – if I, an English person, have been so deeply afflicted, that even this sweet house and society – even my Susan and her lovely children – have been incapable to give me any species of pleasure, or keep me from a desponding low-spiritedness, what must be the feelings of all but the culprits in France!

M. de Narbonne and M. d'Arblay have been almost annihilated: they are for ever repining that they are French, and, though two of the most accomplished and elegant men I ever saw, that break our hearts with the humiliation they feel for their guiltless birth in that guilty country! –'Est-ce vrai,'cries M. de Narbonne, 'que vous conservez encore quelque amitié, M. Lock, pour ceux qui ont la honte et le malheur d'être nés François?' – Poor man! – he has all the symptoms upon him of the jaundice; and M. d'Arblay, from a very fine figure and good face, was changed, as if by magic, in one night, by the receipt of this inexpiable news, into an appearance as black, as meagre, and as miserable as M. de la Blancherie.

We here are all expecting war every day. This dear family has deferred its town journey till next Wednesday. I have not been at all at Mickleham, nor yet settled whether to return to town with the Locks, or to pay my promised visit there first. All has been so dismal, so wretched, that I have scarce ceased to regret our living at such times, and not either sooner or later.

These immediate French sufferers here interest us, and these alone have been able to interest me at all. We hear of a very bad tumult in Ireland, and near Captain Phillip's property: Mr Brabazon writes it is very serious. Heaven guard us from insurrections! What must be the feelings at the Queen's house? how acute, how indignant!

Adieu, most dear sir; I am sure we sympathise but too completely on this subject,

And am ever your

F.B.

LETTERS FROM BATTLE

1799–1805

WILLIAM BURRIDGE
1776–1799

William Burridge, the son of Philip Doble Burridge and Elizabeth Burridge, was born at Stoke Court, Stoke St Mary in 1776. In 1799 he was amongst the Anglo-Russian forces sent to the Netherlands, as was his brother Francis George Burridge. This letter was written from the West Frisian island of Texel, which is separated by a narrow strait from the mainland town of Helder. A note written on the letter by his mother reads, "I think this is the Last that I received from poor Wm".

He died in the following month and is amongst those of his family commemorated on a plaque in the chancel of Stoke Church:

"Capn William Burridge of the 69th Regt of Foot, Son of the said Phillip Doble Burridge – Died at the Helder October 1799 aged 23"

Camp near Theslfelden, off the Texel

Holland

3rd Sept 1799

Dear Mother

I have embraced the first opportunity of sending you a few lines just by way of letting you know I am a live and lusty th'o at the same time have had a near escape. We sailed the next day after I wrote you from the Blanche. Had a bad voyage – seventeen days at sea & no fresh provisions. After the four first days I was very sick & in a high fever – for seven days had no passage through my body. When I was getting better & seem'd to gain an appetite I cou'd get nothing but salt meat to eat of which I cou'd take but little, yet I recovered astonishingly the two last days. We landed in Holland on Tuesday the 27th August at day break. In the morning had an obstinate battle for 7 or 8 hours in which I twice narrowly escaped my life. A shell passed my head within 6 inches & a musket shot passed my face close to my left eye and took off the binding of my hat; but thanks be to God I am alive well & able to tell the story. We had an officer killed, but lost 15 Men in our regt., in the whole I think about 550 and one thousand Dutch but that is my own opinion – for the exact amount I must refer you to the Papers.

After we had buried the Dead we had to sleep on the sand hills where we fought the battle – nothing to cover us from the wind or rain but what we had on our backs and our nose mouth and eyes full of sand. Nothing had we to eat but a ship biscuit and drop of rum for the two first days. The third we got cattle to supply our hunger & was very glad to get a skin for to cover us by night. But luxury must not last for ever for on Saturday I was detached with 24 Men to take care of all the Cattle for the supply of the army where again I had nothing to cover me but the Heavens. Was sent for on Sunday to march where we now are in a Dutch camp which we reached 10 o'clock at night. Just going to lye down when we were ordered to the Town of Helder to relieve an other regt but that was one mile march only. The regt. remained there yesterday but I was sent to the Texel with dispatches from Sir Ralph Ambercrombie to Admiral Mitchel and on my return to e/y Helder was fortunate enough to get a Bed – the second time I have pulled off my clothes since I left England and must not expect to do it again unless we should remove to some Town.

George is well. I met him on our march here, & he was marching from whence we came. We shook hands but cou'd ask no questions. Bryant was with him. I afterwards met Than (?): he told me he had landed only four days – of course saw nothing of the action (n)or did any of the second expedition. George will be able to write me but I don't expect to see him again during the Campaign. We now shall be able to live pretty well; Hares Rabbits & wild fowls are very plenty here. I shot three Rabbits last night. If you should not have received the letter I wrote you from the Blanche, recollect I have left one of my Trunks at a Mr Woottons, Burchington, Isle of Thannett, Kent. He is a Shopkeeper & Taylor. I gave him your address & told him to send it you in the course of six Months if I did not return myself. I think you may as well send for it after that time as I am as likely to land as near Stoke as there. I desired Mr Membry to send you home my great Trunk when the W. Somst regt left Bristol which I thank you to have kept in as dry a place as possible & not opened on any account. I've not received any pay yet or any of my allowances in case I shou'd be popped off. You will have to receive of the Paymaster or Agents something – I rather think a round hundred if we share with the Navy the prize Money for the Forts & Ships we have taken. We don't expect any serious engagement before we come near Amsterdam. I will write you again when I have any thing worth relating. But you must write me soon or tell R. Bullen any thing you wou'd wish to have said, whom I shall desire to write me as often as he can. So must conclude with best love to Brothers & sisters & relations. Comptd to Friends,

your Affect – son W. Burridge

P.S. my present address is . . . . Burridge 69 regt Helder near Texel Holland Take care of Moll

'SAM'

'Sam', surname unknown, was a sailor on board the Royal Sovereign, the flagship of Admiral Collingwood, the second-in-command at the Battle of Trafalgar.

October or November 1805

Honoured Fathre,

This comes to tell you that I am alive and hearty except three fingers; but that's not much, it might have been my head. I told brother Tom I should like to see a greadly battle, and I have seen one, and we have peppered the Combined rarely (off Trafalgar); and for the matter of that, they fought us pretty tightish for French and Spanish. Three of our mess are killed, and four more of us winged. But to tell you the truth of it, when the game began, I wished myself at Warnborough with my plough again; but when they had given us one duster, and I found myself snug and tight, I set to in good earnest, and thought no more about being killed than if I were at Murrell Green Fair, and I was presently as busy and as black as a collier. How my fingers got knocked overboard I don't know, but off they are, and I never missed them till I wanted them. You see, by my writing, it was my left hand, so I can write to you and fight for my King yet. We have taken a rare parcel of ships, but the wind is so rough we cannot bring them home, else I should roll in money, so we are busy smashing 'em and blowing'em up wholesale.

Our dear Admiral Nelson is killed! so we have paid pretty sharply for licking 'em. I never set eyes on him, for which I am both sorry and glad; for to be sure, I should like to have seen him – but then, all the men in our ship are such soft toads, they have done nothing but blast their eyes, and cry, ever since he was killed. God bless you! chaps that fought like the devil, sit down and cry like a wench. I am still in the *Royal Sovereign*, but the Admiral has left her, for she is like a horse without a bridle, so he is in a frigate that he may be here and there and everywhere, for he's as cute as here and there one, and as bold as a lion, for all he can cry! I saw his tears with my own eyes, when the boat hailed and said my Lord was dead. So no more at present from

Your dutiful Son,
Sam

———————————

POETS

1790–1811

MATTHIAS CLAUDIUS
1740–1815

The German poet, Matthias Claudius, was born on the 15th August 1740 in Reinfeld, Holstein and died on the 21st January 1815 in Hamburg. He edited the newspaper *Der Wandsbecker Bothe* from 1771–1775 and wrote a collection of essays, stories, reviews and poems of the same title running to seven volumes. His work is an expression of his personality and bears witness to his child-like and deeply pious humanity. His poem *Der Mond ist aufgegangen (The Moon has risen)* is still one of the best known songs in Germany.

MATTHIAS CLAUDIUS TO HIS SON

7th September 1796

Dear Fritz,

Last week there was a market in Hanover and I asked Herr Wehrs to buy a handsome whip for my Fritz on this market. Tomorrow evening we shall see what he bought and you will see it on Wednesday evening. Until then you will have to make do with the old one. The boys here are so stupid, they don't have whips at all, neither do they ride on horseback but walk everywhere. Adieu, dear Fritz, and on Thursday morning you will have to be so good as to come into my bed and lay in my arms for half an hour.

Adieu,

Yours M.C.

Hamburg
16th August 1803

Dear Anna

Many thanks, dear Anna, for the birthday-cap; we have decided that if Max, as you wrote, had worked on it as well, he must have made the tassel on top. Be that as it may, I put it on immediately, as soon as Caroline and Perthes had delivered it at 10am and paraded in it all day long. The messengers were meant to stay for lunch and a roast and a cake had been prepared for them but little Matthias had another attack of his illness and so they didn't want to be away from him for too long, though they breakfasted off the cake that had just become ready. Why do you have to be 12 miles away on such and similar occasions? Everyone is well here and send their heartfelt greetings to you and Max and the children, especially Mama.

Wandsbeck
5th February 1806

My dear Anna!

So the fear for Caroline is over. You children keep us old ones always warm. If one doesn't love you, it's hardly worthwhile to have children at all, and if one does love you, there is always fear and worry. Well, as it is, we live in the land of fear and worry and so there is relief and a feeling of well-being when, as Socrates said, the chains are loosened. Caroline and her robust, new-born boy are up to extremely well. I represented Max. I don't know whether the boy will have a double beard or none at all; but on that day the representatives had a tough time with their beards. My barber did not turn up and I had to take my beard with me to Hamburg where finally a barber's apprentice from Berlin took pity on it for 2 Schillings. Besser, though by nature already in Hamburg, had a long beard when we arrived and said, when Perthes mentioned it, that surely Max would have turned up with a beard as well and that therefore he couldn't very well not.

Quite a few people in Hamburg have thrown themselves from the 2nd and 3rd floor, because of poverty and neediness. And recently a carpenter's apprentice has been murdered gruesomely and his naked body thrown into the canal. The culprits have been apprehended, though; one had the insolence to sell the murdered man's bloody coat to a Jew and to go out in the same's waistcoat and shirt and even to come to the fair. Another murderer who already received his sentence, is even more insolent and satanic; he curses and blasphemes without shame or embarrassment and regrets that he had not killed the bailiff of Barmbeck who had arrested him, and in this frame of mind he is supposed to be hanged next Monday. If only his heart could be changed; but it is already Wednesday.

God knows that I'd rather tell you of sublime, great deeds and minds; but except for the saints of Tersteegen they are rarely found in these parts and according to the newspapers they don't seem to be plentiful around you either. The mistake is probably partly that we always expect others to improve instead of starting with ourselves.

Yours M.C.

TO HIS DAUGHTER CAROLINE AND HIS SON-IN-LAW PERTHES

Dear, dear Line and dear Perthes,

I keep thanking you and thanking you without ever getting anywhere because when I think that I have dried off my head from the waters of your generosity, you pour another lake of it over nose and ears, so that in the end I just lie in it quietly because there is no hope of ever getting out of it. The settee is perfect and excellent; what can we say. I shall lie on it often and think of you and pray that God be good to you.

Adieu. Adieu. M.C.

LORD BYRON
1788–1824

George Gordon Byron, the poet, was the son of Captain John Byron and Catherine Gordon of Gight. He was sent to school at Harrow where the following letter was written to his mother who doted upon her only son. He was born with a club foot which is generally supposed to have had some bearing on his future flamboyant character. The shoes which were made especially for him were thus particularly important – hence the reference to Sheldrake. Newstead, which he refers to, is Newstead Abbey in Nottinghamshire which he inherited with the baronetcy in 1798.

In this letter the 15 year old Lord Byron is much aggrieved by his victimisation by one his tutors, Mr Henry Drury, the son of Dr Drury, the Headmaster, whom Byron evidently respects.

Harrow-on-the Hill,
Sunday, May 1st, 1803.

My dear Mother,

I received your Letter the other day. And am happy to hear you are well. I hope you will find Newstead in as favorable a state as you can wish. I wish you would write to Sheldrake to tell him to make haste with my shoes.

I am sorry to say that Mr Henry Drury has behaved himself to me in a manner I neither *can* nor *will bear*. He has seized now an opportunity of showing his resentment towards me. To day in church I was talking to a Boy who was sitting next me; *that* perhaps was not right, but hear what followed. After Church he spoke not a word to me, but he took this Boy to his pupil room, where he abused me in a most violent manner, called me *blackguard*, said he *would* and *could* have me expelled from the School, and bade me thank his *Charity* that *prevented* him; this was the Message he sent me, to which I shall return no answer, but submit my case to *you* and those you may think *fit* to *consult*. Is this fit usage for any body? had I *stole* or behaved in the most *abominable* way to him, his language could not have been more outrageous. What must the boys think of me to hear such a Message ordered to be delivered to me by a *Master*? Better let him take away my life that ruin my *Character*. My Conscience acquits me of ever *meriting* expulsion at this School; I have been *idle* and I certainly ought not to talk in church, but I have never done a mean action at this School to him or *any one*. If I had done anything so *heinous*, why should he allow me to stay at the School? Why should he himself be so *criminal* as to overlook faults which merit the *appellation* of a *blackguard*? If he had had it in his power to have me expelled he would long ago have *done* it; as it is, he had done *worse*. If I am treated in this Manner, I will not stay at this *School*. I write you that I will not as yet appeal to Dr. Drury; his Son's influence is more that mine and *justice* would be *refused* me. Remember I told you, when I *left* you at Bath, that he would seize every means and opportunity of revenge, not for leaving him so much as the mortification he suffered, because I begged you to let me leave him. If I had been the Blackguard he talks of, why did he not of his own accord refuse to keep me as his *pupil?* You know Dr. Drury's first letter, in it were these Words: 'My son and Lord Byron have had some Dis-agreements; but I hope that his future behaviour will render a change of Tutors unnecessary.' Last Term I was here but a short time, and though he endeavoured, he could find nothing to abuse me in. Among other things I forgot to tell you he said he had a great mind to expel the Boy for speaking to me, and that if he ever again spoke to me he would expel him. Let him explain his meaning; he abused me, but neither did nor can mention anything bad of me, further than what every boy else in the School has done. I fear him not; but let him explain his meaning; 'tis all I ask. I beg you will write to Dr. Drury to let him know what I have said. He has behaved to me, as also Mr. Evans, very kindly. If you do not take notice of this, I will leave the School myself; but I am sure *you* will not see me *ill-treated*; better that I should suffer anything than this. I believe you will be tired by this time of reading my letter, but, if you love me, you will now show it. Pray write me immediately. I shall ever remain,

Your affectionate Son,

Byron.

PS. Hargreaves Hanson desires his love to you and hopes you are very well. I am not in want of any Money so will not ask you for any. God bless, bless you.

PERCY BYSSHE SHELLEY
1792–1822

Shelley's conventional upbringing helped to make him, as a young man, deeply unhappy and rebellious. He went to University College Oxford where he was consciously eccentric and was sent down in 1811 for circulating a provocative pamphlet.

This letter is written to his 60 year old father, from York, on the 12th October 1811. Shelley is 20 years old and has just unsuccessfully asked his father for some money. He is definitely in his father's bad books for not only turning his back on Christianity, but for eloping with a sixteen year old schoolgirl.

Dear Father

The waggoner has written to inform me that my property is sent – but does it not look as if your resentment was not to be supported by reason that you have declined to write yourself?

I cannot avoid thinking thus, nor expressing my opinion; but silence, especially on so important a subject as I urged, looks as if you confessed the erroneousness of your proceedings, at the same time that your passions impel you to persist in them. I do not say this is illiberal, a person who can once persuade himself as you have done that every opinion adopted by the majority is correct, must be nearly indifferent to this charge; I do not say it is immoral, as illiberality involves a portion of immorality, but it is emphatically hostile to your own interest, to the opinion which the world will form of your virtues. *If you are a professor of Christianity, which I am not,* I need not recall to your recollection "Judge not lest thou should'st be judged."

I confess I write this more to discharge a duty of telling you what I think, than hoping that my representations will be effectual. We have taken widely different views of the subject in question. *Obedience* is in my opinion a word which should have no existence – you regard it as necessary.–

Yes, you can command it. The institutions of society have made you, tho' liable to be misled by passion and prejudice like others, the *Head of the family*; and I confess it is almost natural for minds not of the highest order to value even the errors whence they derive their importance.

Adieu, answer this.–

I would be your aff. dut. Son

Percy B. Shelley

VICTORIAN ENGINEERS

1824–1863

GEORGE STEPHENSON
1781–1848

ROBERT STEPHENSON
1804–1859

George and Robert Stephenson were part of that new section of society which included engineers and scientists who transformed the world with the industrial revolution. George and Robert Stephenson, together with Brunel, were responsible for the development of railways. George Stephenson was an entirely self-made man, leaving at his death in 1848 the considerable sum of £140,000. He was born in 1781 in a mining village in Northumbria. He had no formal education and started work at the age of 8 keeping the cows off the horse-drawn tramway at the local colliery. When he was 10 he went to work full-time in the colliery. There he developed an aptitude for repairing and inventing machines, and eventually became colliery engineer. Gradually George gained a reputation for building railways and engines for collieries and in 1825 was responsible for building the world's first public railway between Stockton and Darlington.

Robert Stephenson was born in 1804, and followed his father's enthusiasm for engineering. In order to gain experience Robert went to South America for three years as mining engineer to the Columbian Mining Association. Before leaving for South America, Robert, aged 20, visited various engineering works in Wales and the West Country, details of which he enthusiastically reported back to his father in this letter from Devon (now in the archives of the Institution of Civil Engineers). On his return from South America Robert, initially in association with his father, became a famous, and wealthy, railway engineer. His achievements include the London–Birmingham railway and the magnificent tubular Britannia bridge across the Menai Straits. He died in October 1859, a few days after his friend Isambard Kingdom Brunel. Such was his fame that he was buried in Westminster Abbey; The Queen expressed her personal regrets and in consideration of Robert's "world wide fame" and the "country's great loss" allowed the cortege to pass through Hyde Park to the Abbey.

Oakhampton

8 March 1824

My dear Father,

As I have proceeded in my journey to the Cornish mines I have every reason to think that it will not be mispent time for when one is travelling about something new generally presents itself and though it is perhaps not superior to some scheme of our own for the same purpose, it seldom fails to open a new channel of ideas which may not infrequently prove advantageous in the end, this I think is one of the chief benefits of leaving for awhile the Fireside where the young imagination received its first impressions.

We were part of a day at Bristol where I made a tour through the Steam Boats which were all except one laid up for the Winter. I was in the *George 4th* the packet you and I came from Ireland in and I was surprised to find that they have removed the parallel motion. The Engineman told me that they were taking the parallel motions off every one of them as they were found entirely superflous. I was in two other Boats which had also undergone the same alterations. I was informed that nearly all the Boats were laying off the Trail or connecting Link between the two Cranks as they found that the crank pin working loose into one of the Cranks obviated a considerable degree of friction. I saw one Crank pin upon which had been working one of those Trail Links and it was not less than 1/8 of an inch guttered on one side. This was evidently owing to the crank bearings yielding but if it had been a loose eyed crank it would have accomodated itself to this yielding of the Machinery. I think we must put the simple crank in the Stockton Steamboat.

I have been at Swansea and went through their works. They seem to be going on very well. The Engine you put up to draw coals is going admirably and I dare say is making a tolerable good vacuum altho' only working from the bottom side of the plunger. I see they have got our patent Airpump into the Repertory of Arts this last month. I was all through the Neath Abbey works but you have been there. I need say nothing about them for they are considerably behind us in the fitting up department, and it is my opinion that this Mexican contract will be a loosing job for them; indeed the Engine builders in this neighbourhood as far as I can learn, care little about their profits if they can just make ends meet. Mr. Price shewed me a 70 inch cylinder Engine which they were fitting up for Cornwall and he told me that he was ashamed to mention the price only he could assure me it would not return an old penny for a new one. When I was at Neath Abbey I had the pleasure of being introduced to Mr. Brunton the Engineer, he is a very sensible man but there is none of them understands the Parallel motion thoroughly, they seem to doubt me when I told them I had never seen one mathematically true not even in principle. I have found since I left home that even in the case where all the bars are equal its not true exactly. I know you will doubt it but this is true.

Yours most Faithfully

Robert Stephenson

(My Uncle & I are both well)

In 1827 George Stephenson was appointed Engineer to the Liverpool–Manchester Railway, with a salary of £1000. He was by now a very successful engineer and his services were much in demand by the rapidly developing railway companies. Because of his lack of formal education, much of his business correspondence was largely dictated to secretaries. This letter is one of the longest written in his own hand and is to Robert, who was still working as a mining engineer in Columbia. It was analysed by Professor Simmons and quoted in Hunter Davies' biography of George Stephenson. The spelling is largely phonetic, based on the way he must have spoken; some punctuation and paragraphs have been added to make it easier to read. The letter is much concerned with family matters but he cannot avoid discussing engineering with a fellow engineer. Part of the letter refers to his progress and confidence in crossing Chat Moss, one of the triumphs of Nineteenth Centuary civil engineering and a task considered impossible by many of his contempories.

GEORGE STEPHENSON TO HIS SON ROBERT

Leverpool

Feb 23rd 1827

My Dear

Robert your very welcom letter dated Oct 26 we duly received and was glad to here such good newes from Columbia respecting the mines – but at the same time greatly disapointed at you not getting home so soon as was expected. however I can hope all will be for the best, and I must waddle on as well as I can untill you get to join me. There has been a florishing a count of your men in the English pappers and great creadit is given to Robert

Stephenson for his good management of them.

I must now let you know how we are geting on in this quarter. Yore mother is getting her tea beside me while I am riting this and in good spirits. she has been in Leverpool a bout a fortnight. We have a very comfortable home, and a Roume set a side for Robert and Charels when they arive in England.

We are getting rapitly on with the tunnal under Liverpool it is 22 feet width & 16 feet high we have 6 shafts and driving right & left we have also got a great deal done on chat moss and on the same plans that I prepared befor parlament 2 years a go which plans was condemed by almost all the Engineers in England. these plans is by cutting & inbanking with the moss some of the laths 12 feet high and stand remarkably well – . . . .

> *He then goes on to discuss some of his other engineering projects and ideas, comments on the progress of the tunnel under the Thames at Rotherhithe by another father and son partnership, Marc Isambard Brunel and Isambard Kingdom Brunel.*

I think the projected tunnal under the thames was talked of befor you left – it is now got a good way under the river but will cost a great deal more money than was expected. This is however a very common case with engineers – the estimate for this concern is 500000£, and I daresay it will require it all.

> *Finally, he returns to family concerns.*

. . . . you may depend upon it that if you do not get home soon every thing will be at perfection and then there will be nothing for you to do or invent – however we will hope that some usfull Ideas will be brought from the western world. . . .

. . . . your mother expects you will not forget the presents. you must bring more than one as Mrs Robert Stephenson will want one by & by – and we expect Mr. Charels will bring plenty of amarica plant seeds for our (garden). cannot you bring your favorate mule with you. I trust this letter will just catch you befor leaving the country. my kindest love to Charels I am my Dear Dear Robert your affectionate father Goe : Stephenson

THOMAS CASEBOURNE
1797–1864

Thomas Casebourne was born in 1797 at Hemel Hempstead, Herts, and was a favourite pupil of Thomas Telford by whom he was employed as assistant on several works. He was in charge of the execution of the works of the Ulster Canal which was designed by Telford to link the west and the north of Ireland. In 1845 he became the Resident Engineer of the Harbour and Docks at West Hartlepool. He was elected an Associate of the Institution of Civil Engineers 1828 and a Member in 1837. He died in 1864 at the age of 66. In an obituary written at the time it was stated that "he was a careful, conscientious man, had a good knowledge of the practice of Civil Engineering, and very deservedly, acquired the confidence of all with whom he was brought into contact."

This letter, to his son, the engineer C.T. Casebourne, illustrates the trust that must have been put in the postal service of the time. It is most probable that the letter written on a Sunday afternoon was delivered the same day.

West Hartlepool
Sunday Afternoon 28 June 1863

My dear Charley

I don't know how it came to pass that I should have altogether forgotten when we met this morning, to offer you what I do most sincerely wish, the usual congratulations upon this the return of your natal day.

I now take this present mode of communicating my feelings, and I hope it will make up for the least anxiety, which may in the interim, have foreshadowed any want of love or affection either to yourself or your dear spouse.

May you both be spared to spend many happy years together.
Your sincere and affectionate father
Thos. Casebourne.

COMPOSERS AND WRITERS

1824–1873

HECTOR BERLIOZ
1803–1869

In 1821 Hector Berlioz went to Paris to follow his father by becoming a medical student. He had no desire to do this. As he wrote in his Memoirs,

"Become a doctor! Study anatomy! Dissect! Take part in horrible operations – instead of giving myself body and soul to music, sublime art whose grandeur I was beginning to perceive! Forsake the highest heaven for the wretchedest regions of the earth, the immortal spirits of poetry and their divinely inspired strains for dirty hospital orderlies, dreadful dissecting-room attendants, hideous corpses, the screams of patients, the groans and rattling breath of the dying!

No, no! It seemed to me the reversal of the whole natural order of my existence. It was monstrous. It could not happen. Yet it did."

This caused consternation in the family and much anguished correspondence between Hector and his father, which led to Hector's magnificent statement of the credo of the artist, included in the first of the letters selected. Gradually Dr Berlioz became reconciled to his son's chosen career as a composer, though unfortunately he never heard any of his music performed. The letters vividly demonstrate the dilemma of a middle class family when a son chooses not follow the normal establishment behaviour and enter one of the acceptable professions, but insists on becoming an artist. These letters also contain the perennial requests from children to parents for money, and, endearingly, a request to mother for no more handkerchiefs, please but something useful like stockings.

Paris
31 August 1824

My dear Papa,

I need not tell you how much your letter surprised and hurt me; you your-self can be in no doubt of it, and I dare to hope your heart disavows the wounding remarks it contained. I do not understand either how the letter I left for Alphonse can have roused you to such a point; it contained nothing, I think, that I haven't said or communicated to you a hundred times, nor do I believe that in speaking of my parents I let fall any expression inconsistent with the feelings of a loving and respectful son.

I am driven involuntarily towards a magnificent career – no other adjec-tive can be applied to the career of an artist – and not towards my doom. For I believe I shall succeed; yes, I believe it. There is no point in being modest about it. To prove to you that I am not simply trusting to luck, I think, I am convinced that I shall achieve distinction in music. All outward signs encour-age me to believe so, and the voice of nature within me speaks louder than the most rigorous dictates of reason. . . .

That is the way I think, that is the way I am, and nothing in the world will change me. You could withdraw all support from me and force me to leave Paris; but I do not believe it, you would not wish to make me lose the best years of my life – to break the magnetic needle because you can't stop it obeying the attraction of the poles.

Farewell, dear Papa; read my letter again, and do not attribute it to momentary excitement. I have never been calmer.

I embrace you tenderly, as well as Mama and my sisters.

Your respectful and loving son,
H. Berlioz

Paris, 1828

. . . . Thank you, dear Mama, for the handkerchiefs you sent me by Charles. But actually they're what I'm in need of least. What I am short of are stockings. I've not got one whole pair, and every day the number that are wearable diminishes. Please send me some whenever you can.

So Grandfather's made up his mind to come and visit you? Tell my sisters

to give him my love.
Farewell, my dear Mama, I embrace you tenderly.
Your loving son
H. Berlioz

TO HIS FATHER

10 May 1830

My excellent father,
How grateful I am for your letter! It has done me much good. So you are beginning to feel a little confidence in me. May I justify it! It's the first time you have written to me like that, and I can't thank you enough. It is a great happiness to be able to give pleasure and do honour to those one loves. Yes, indeed, I should be delighted if you could hear me. But for a journey to Paris, something more certain and definite is needed than a concert which can be cancelled at the whim of the authorities. For the past week I've been waiting, with intense impatience, for permission from M. Mangin the chief of police to advertise the concert.

I'm already following your instructions as to regime. I normally eat little and have virtually given up tea. For the past few days I've done nothing except correct orchestral parts, keep an eye on my copyists, and copy parts myself. In the evening I go to the German theatre, where the director has been so courteous as to give me a free pass without my having to ask for one. I'm counting on the fabulous Haitzinger to sing at my concert and complete the programme.

Rome
18th February 1832

I was on the point of writing to you, dear Father, when your letter arrived. It aroused in me a mass of disturbing and painful thoughts. I see you so sad, so unhappy, from a thousand causes that you had no reason to expect. My sister's marriage itself, by separating her from you, must have made your solitude more grievous and profound. Nanci was not the one of the family who understood you least well, and I fear that though you don't mention it such as separation has cost you a great deal.

Berlioz goes on to discuss the problems of Prosper his brother and it prompts him to unburden himself frankly on a number of topics, including education, money and marriage.

My ideas on education are very different from yours, I think I can say so openly without fear of displeasing you. I consider French provincial education, for many children, totally absurd. Parents have only two careers in view, law and medicine; but even when they have no clear, decided objective for their sons they persist just the same in making them waste – I use the word deliberately – the ten best years of their life in the mire of a college learning a dead language which they will never master. What is the use of even knowing Latin very well – except to qualify for one of the two faculties? A young man who has learnt English and German, who from an early age is involved in what's going on around him, without troubling himself what the Greeks and Romans did, a young man who has been in a position to observe, from an early age, the world with which he will have to deal, not an extinct world which is of no interest to him, is a thousand times better placed to get on and find his natural level. For politics, diplomacy, travel, the navy, the arts, literature, business, even the exact sciences, it's clear that nowadays we have to begin by being able to communicate freely with the great centres of civilisation which adjoin ours. The rest comes later and is learned much better.

. . . . Children reason little; but they feel the inopportuneness of certain things. I remember clearly that from the first I was convinced that I should never be a doctor. If instead of struggling so long I had been free to set my own course and deploy all my faculties as later I was to do, I should be not five but ten years further on.

Now, to turn to me. After my last letter had gone I feared that what I had replied to Mama on the subject of money might have upset you and I regretted having let it slip. But since you broach it it's better I should speak frankly. I genuinely believed that the income of a thousand francs which you promised me at the time when it was a question of my getting married would still be mine on my remaining a bachelor, especially since you never said anything to the contrary. I made arrangements accordingly, never imagining for a moment that you needed the money. When Mama, in sending it to me, chided me a little – very gently and indulgently, I must say – I felt I was back under the old system which I always found so tormenting, when I was kept on a leash, and I admit it came as a shock to me. Its better I should say so and be quite open about it. Every compulsory restraint, every obvious bridle, everything that threatens my freedom in the least degree, is unendurable to me. I have suffered terribly the past eight years, the most recent period of my life is a sad story of which you know only a few minor episodes, and which has formed my character as it is today. I am like someone who has been flayed. Every part of me has become excruciatingly sensitive so that I howl at the slightest touch. As a result, I should infinitely rather be short of money than have it at that cost. Five hundred francs agreed and settled would I swear be worth more to me than five thousand that I had to obtain by degrees, irregularly, complete with criticisms etc. Besides, now that I know for a fact that you would be going short on my account, I don't wish to hear any more about it. My personal expenses are not great, and with my grant I should not have needed anything, but for the trip to Naples that I had just made. The sole privations I experience for lack of money are to do with my art; it is only for that that I should like to be rich, so as to be able to exert my musical powers sooner and on a larger scale.

You talk of marriage, I have no ideas on the subject that would take us far, too far for me to express them freely here. It's enough to tell you that at present I'm not in the least inclined to it. I'm only too well aware that an ordinary marriage, what is called a sensible marriage, a placid, *reasonable* marriage, would be the death . . . .

TO HIS FATHER

Paris,
April 18??

. . . . The 200 francs which you kindly sent me at the beginning of the month won't last beyond the 3rd or 4th of May, as I was obliged to give 50 fr. which were overdue for manuscript paper and copying that I had to pay for. Then I bought a hat which cost me 20 fr. I had my boots repaired for 14 fr. And I had two pairs of shoes made, 14 fr. I am also going to make a request, my dear Papa, which may strike you as tactless. I have an intense desire to acquire the complete works of Volney, made up, as you know, of the *Ruins, Travels in Syria*, the *Description of the United States*, the *Letters on Greece*, and the *Researches into Ancient History*. This superb edition, the only one that exists, is

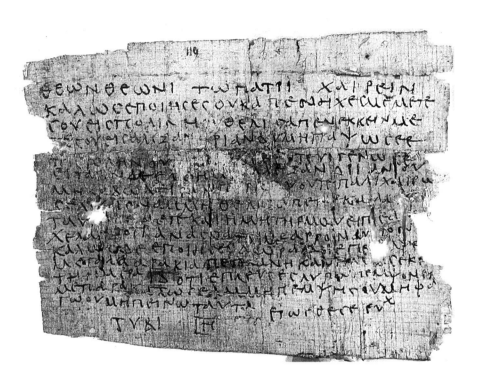

Letter written on papyrus from Theon to his father in the second century A. D.
Written from Oxyrhnchus

I

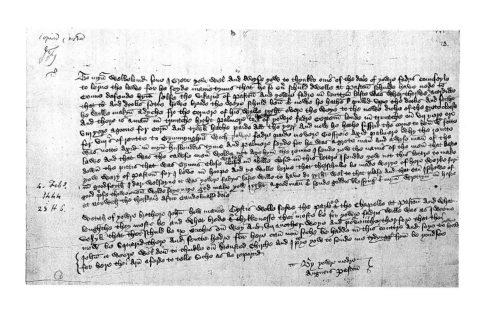

Letter written in English from Agnes Paston to one of her sons, 4th February 1444

Letter written in Latin from Prince Edward (later to become King Edward IV) to his father King Henry VIII. Written from Hatfield House.

Si filiorum pietas omnibus officijs parentes suos psequi debet venerande pater, non sum adeo teneræ ætatis quin possim intelligere officium meum esse omnibus modis gratificari maiestati tuæ: non solum quia pater es, sed quia pater pientissimus, et filij tui amantissimus. Quare cum nullum adhuc aliud officium pietati tuæ præstare possim præter salutationes, idq per literas non per sermonem: visum est iterum scribere. Peto autem a celsitudine tua benedictionem mihi impertiri. Vt videre celsitudinem tuam gestio, sic non importune peto, nisi celsitudini tuæ placuerit. Opto deniq atq oro deum, vt diutissime ac felicissime viuat tua maiestas,

Maiestatis tuæ filius obsequentissimus
Edouardus Princeps.

Painting of Edward VI by unknown artist

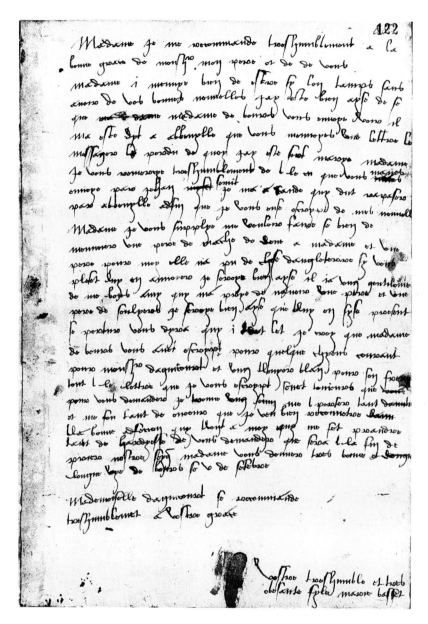

Letter written in French from Mary Basset to her mother, Lady Lisle

Note scribbled on the inside of an envelope from Thackeray to his mother

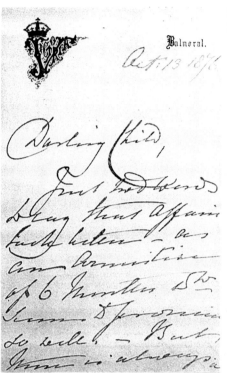

Fragment of letter from Queen Victoria to her eldest daughter, Victoria

Queen Victoria writing letters attended by her Indian servant, Abdul Karim

Photograph of Herbert
Levy leaving Germany by
Kinderstransport (1939)

My dear all!
Because Mama wrote yesterday a letter
to you, she can not write this week. We have received the nice parcel and thank you so much. Mama
was very glad about all the things and will write
next week. Please tell to everyone also to aunt
Gisa our thanks. Please send with the other things
a brush for cleaning suits in our room in the cupboard and Knopflochgummi. It is in Mamas Needelwork-
basket. Mama has a nice birthday to day. Now we was
in the cinema. Kisses. Herbert

Port Erin 9.7.1940

Herbert Levy's first
card written in
English to his
parents whilst on
holiday in Port Erin

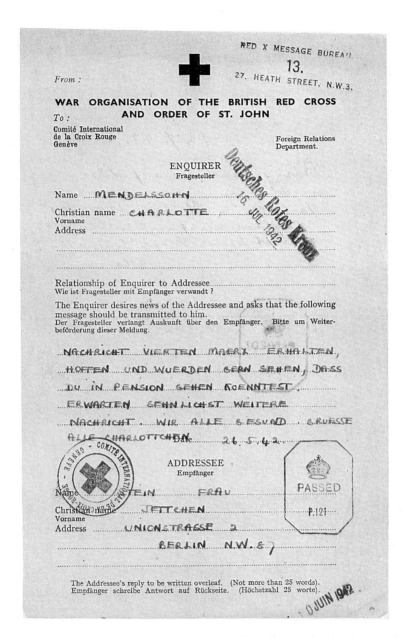

Red Cross letter from Herbery Levy's aunt living in London to his grandmother living in Berlin

on the point of going out of print, the Government has forbidden a reprinting, and the price is rising all the time. Three months ago it was selling for 40 fr., at the moment it can't be had for less then 64, and in spite of this there are only twenty copies left.

Farewell, dear Papa, please believe that I am not so far from being what you wish me to be, and that one day I will make you amends for the pain I have caused you.

Your respectful and loving son,

H. Berlioz

WILLIAM WORDSWORTH
1770–1850

William Wordsworth was educated at Hawkshead Grammar School and then St Johns College, Cambridge. After coming down in 1790 he spent a year in France during the onset of the French Revolution. During this time he fell in love with the daughter of a surgeon at Blois, Annette Vallon, and they had a daughter, Caroline. William then returned to England full of revolutionary ideas, but he was to stay in touch with Annette and his daughter, visiting them and making sure that they were provided for.

In 1802 he married Mary Hutchinson. She was a member of a large family who had long been friends of the Wordsworths. William and Mary eventually made their home in Grasmere in the Lake District with Dorothy, William's sister. Mary and William had five children and according to diaries, letters and journals of the time, theirs was a hospitable home, always welcoming extra guests.

William was particularly close to his daughter Dora. She attended school at Ambleside and spent a great deal of time with her father, accompanying him on walks, particularly when he was worried about losing his sight after his periodic bouts of trachoma. He addressed many of his poems to her such as *"A little onward lend thy guiding hand"*. So devoted was he that he bought some land at Rydal Mount which he gave to Dora and called it *Dora's Field* and when Dora went to stay in Cambridge and needed her pony, a servant took it as far as Lancaster, but it was William who rode it the rest of the way so that she should not be without it.

At the age of 27 Dora accompanied him on a Scottish tour to visit Sir Walter Scott. In his book *A Wordsworth Companion* F.B.Pinion describes her "of independent judgment, whose fun and awareness of the incongruous in no way lessened her deep attachment to her father; he doted on her, worried about her health, and loved her blithe spirit." In 1839 Dora became engaged to Edward Quillinan, a widower and old friend of the family. William was shocked, partly because he didn't want to lose her and also because he knew that Quillinan, a poet, could not afford the kind of home and attention that Dora, with her delicate constitution needed. The marriage took place two years later, but Mary and William couldn't bring themselves to attend. In 1847 Dora died of consumption.

In 1850 when William was 80 years old and dying of pleurisy, Mary said to him one evening, "William, you are going to Dora." He did not seem to hear, but the next morning, when his niece entered his room, he asked, "Is that Dora?" It was the day of his death, 23 April.

WILLIAM WORDSWORTH TO HIS DAUGHTER, DORA

Sunday morning, 9 o'clock
9 June 1839

My dearest Dora,

I am looking for Mr Quillinan every moment. I hope to revive the conversation of yesterday.

The sum is: I make no opposition to this marriage. I have no resentment connected with it toward any one: you know how much friendship I have always felt towards Mr Q., and how much I respect him. I do not doubt the strength of his love and affection towards you; this, as far as I am concerned, is the fair side of the case.

On the other hand, I cannot think of parting with you with that complacency, that satisfaction, that hopefulness which I could wish to feel; there is too much of necessity in the case for my wishes. But I must submit, and do submit; and God Almighty bless you, my dear child, and him who is the object of your long and long-tried preference and choice.

Ever your affectionate father,
Wm. Wordsworth.

The following 'little story' reveals a lot about the Wordsworths – William's sensitivity and concern and his wife's immediate and practical response. William then wrote to Dora enlisting her help.

7th April 1840

. . . .Yesterday I dined with Mrs Luff, after calling at the house high up Loughrigg side where dwells the good woman who lost her two children in the flood last winter. The wind was high when I knocked at her door, and I heard a voice from within that I knew not what to make of, though it sounded something like the lullaby of a Mother to her Baby. After entering I found it came from a little sister of those drowned Children, that was singing to a bundle of clouts, rudely put together to look like a Doll, which she held in her arms.

I tell you this little story in order that, if it be perfectly convenient, but on no account else, you may purchase what may answer the purpose with something more of pride and pleasure to this youngling of a nurse. Such is your mother's wish, I should not have had the wit to think of it. No matter, she says, how common a sort of thing the doll is, only let it be a good big one.

GUSTAVE FLAUBERT
1821–1880

The Flaubert family, like Dr Berlioz, found it very difficult to come to terms with a son who would not do the normal, sensible thing and enter a respectable, safe and well-paid profession. The son of a provincial doctor, Gustave Flaubert grew up in a house where science was considered the most important thing. His elder brother became a doctor and Gustave was destined for the law. Even after giving up his law studies, Flaubert continued to receive advice that he must have a normal job, but the advice was ignored, as with Berlioz a few years earlier.

In 1846 his father died and a few months later his sister, Caroline, also died from an infection contracted during childbirth. From then on Flaubert, his mother and Caroline's baby lived together at Croisset. In 1850 Flaubert embarked on a journey to Egypt and the Middle East where he had long been wanting to go. He kept in touch with his mother by letter.

GUSTAVE FLAUBERT TO HIS MOTHER

Cairo

5 January 1850

Your fine long letter of the 16th reached me as a New Year's present last Wednesday, dear old darling. I was paying an official call on our consul, when he was handed a large packet. He opened it immediately, and I seized the envelope that I recognized among a hundred others. (I was itching to open it, but manners, alas! forbade.) Fortunately, he showed us into his wife's salon, and as there was a letter for her too, from her mother, we gave each other mutual permission to read almost before saying how do you do. . . .

Between Minia and Assiut
23 February 1850

Now I come to something that you seem to enjoy reverting to and that I utterly fail to understand. You are never at a loss for things to torment yourself about. What is the sense of this: that I must have a job – "a small job," you say. First of all, what job? I defy you to find me one, to specify in what field, or what it would be like. Frankly, and without deluding yourself, is there a single one that I am capable of filling? You add: "One that wouldn't take up much of your time and wouldn't prevent you from doing other things." There's the delusion! That's what Bouilhet told himself when he took up medicine, what I told myself when I began law, which nearly brought about my death from suppressed rage. When one does something, one must do it wholly and well. Those bastard experiences where you sell suet all day and write poetry at night are made for mediocre minds – like those horses equally good for saddle and carriage – the worst kind, that can neither jump a ditch nor pull a plough.

In short, it seems to me that one takes a job for money, for honours, or as an escape from idleness. Now you'll grant me darling, (1) that I keep busy enough not to have to go out looking for something to do; and (2) if it's a question of honours, my vanity is such that I'm incapable of feeling myself honoured by anything: a position, however high it may be (and that isn't the kind you speak of) will never give me the satisfaction that I derive from my self-respect when I have accomplished something well in my own way; and finally, if it's not for money, any jobs or job that I could have would bring in too little to make much difference to my income. Weigh all those considerations: *don't knock your head against a hollow idea.* Is there any position in which I'd be closer to you, more yours? And isn't not to be bored one of the principal goals of life? . . . .

And in another letter written in the same year from Constantinople, he replies to his mother who has asked him whether he plans to get married. He finishes the letter, having passionately stated that he intends always to live alone, with the following tender words:

. . . .The devil take me if I know why I've written you these two pages of tirade, poor dear. No, no: when I think of your sweet face, so sad and loving, and of the joy I have in living with you, who are so full of serenity and such grave charm, I know very well that I shall never love another woman as I do you. You will have no rival, never fear! The senses or a momentary fancy will not take the place of what lies locked in the fastness of a triple sanctuary . . . .

JOHANNES BRAHMS
1833–1897

Another mother concerned with the lack of a proper job for her artistic son, was Frau Brahms, who continued to offer her son advice on seeking ways, other than by composition, of earning a living. Again, as with the advice of Mme. Flaubert, it was ignored. This letter was written during the two years that Brahms looked after Robert and Clara Schumann and their seven children in Dusseldorf after Schumann's attempted suicide. Brahms was then aged 20. His friendship with the Schumanns was one of the most important things to have happened to the young Brahms. Clara used to play his compositions and Robert would introduce him to influential figures. Brahms adored the children, to whom he later dedicated his *Album of Children's Folk Songs*. In the following letter, his mother writes in a worried fashion about his staying with the family and how she thinks that he should get on and do something with his life.

FRAU BRAHMS TO HER SON

1854

. . . .Schumann smoothed the way for you but you must do more. You could not live by composing alone – the greatest masters were not able to do it. Hopefully, you would have undertaken something if Schumann had not fallen ill. For the moment you did the right thing in going there. But to remain? You're losing money and time . . . . Like it or not, only the man who has money will be respected.

That you are giving lessons is probably good; at least it's something. But you always disliked it and it brings in very little – I mean for you, who can do so much more. Frau Schumann also gives lessons, but she prefers concertising. Otherwise she wouldn't do it – turn her family and home over to strangers and travel about without a husband. . . . When one has been so richly endowed by God with so many gifts, it's not right to remain sitting there so calmly. . . .

PIOTR ILYICH TCHAIKOVSKY
1840–1893

Tchaikovsky, like Brahms, was late starter. It was not until he was 23 that he decided to make music his career. There was no music in his family, his parents neither understood nor liked music and cultural influences on him as a boy were nil. His father was an inspector of mines in Votinsk, a small town in the Ural mountains. He took piano lessons as a child but he showed no special talent. Later, the family moved to St Petersburg and at 19 Piotr Tchaikovsky entered the Ministry of Justice as Clerk Grade One. To relieve the monotony of the job he did a course in choral singing. He enjoyed it so much that he then decided to try piano lessons again and gradually became interested in composition. He was by now leading a rich cultural life and in 1861 he had the opportunity to travel to Europe.

TO HIS FATHER, ILYA PETROVICH TCHAIKOVSKY

London
29 July –10 August 1861
Dear Papasha!
. . . . We took rooms in a small hotel and spent all our days touring the town. Have just come back from Westminster Abbey and the Houses of Parliament. Yesterday and the day before we spent at the Crystal Palace. The building is really magnificent but inside there is a bit too much colour. We also went into the Thames tunnel where I nearly fainted for lack of air. But I would have passed the time even better if I had not been worried without news from you. London is very interesting but leaves a dark impression on one's soul. One never sees the sun, and it rains all the time . . . .
Your devoted son
P Tchaikovsky

In 1863, at the age of 23 and after endless dithering, Tchaikovsky gave up his job at the Ministry and enrolled as a pupil with Anton Rubinstein, pianist, composer and founder-director of the St Petersburg Conservatoire. His family were shocked but allowed him a small allowance. He completed his course two years later, winning the silver medal for composition.

The symphony he refers to in the next two letters is his Second.

Moscow

22 November 1872

My dearest Golubchik Papochka,

Although you do not openly blame me for not writing more often I still torture myself and am sure you are angry with me. Forgive me my dearest, you know how lazy I am at letter writing. Also, I have been working hard at my symphony which I have now finished, thank God. All the same it is your own fault that you have such lazy sons – blame yourself! And so I cover with loving kisses your grey head, and your hands, and once more beg forgiveness for my laziness.

You say in your letter you hope my flat is warm. Well, up till now I am perfectly satisfied with it. Besides, the weather at present is so warm here that it is even annoying. One wishes for nice crisp frosts instead of misty, damp rainy days! I stay at home quite a lot but go for long walks. If I do not do so my belly will grow enormous and that God forbid! Now that I have finished my symphony I am resting. . . . .

My health is in order, only my eyes worry me a little; they are strained by hard work and my sight has weakened so much, compared to what it used to be that I have acquired a pince-nez. People say it suits me greatly. My nerves are not in order, but nothing can be done about it – anyway this is not important. Who in our position has got good nerves, especially artists!

. . . . My symphony is going to be played in Petersburg and I wish very much that you could hear it. Good–bye, my Golubchik, I kiss your hands and eyes and also hug the 'Bun'*. My Misha begs to give you his humble regards.

P. Tchaikovsky

Lisaveta Mikhailovna–Tchaikovsky's step-mother.

Moscow
5 February 1873

My dear Papochka!

. . . . My symphony was played here last week with great success; I was called for many times and cheered repeatedly. The success was so great that the symphony is going to be played again at the tenth concert and a subscription has been started to make me a present. Also I received 300 roubles from the Musical Society. . . .

Your loving son
Piotr Tchaikovsky

Moscow
9 October 1873

My dear Papochka!

I am deeply ashamed and kiss your dear cheeks and hands and beg again to be forgiven for being so lazy. However, I think you will understand: I get so tired. I have so much to do that when I return home to rest there is no energy left for letter writing; these last days I have not been well. My throat was sore, I had a temperature, and I am still bothered by a nasty cough. But none of this is really serious and otherwise my health is good. Life goes on as usual. There is no time to be bored, but I would be happier if I had some news about my opera. I have just heard that there is nothing certain and it may not be played this season; but I am so sick of waiting and also need the money.

I am like a mother who hopes to get her daughters married and looks everywhere for the most eligible suitors. Not only do I want to hear my opera performed, but I would like, above all, to pass three or four weeks in Petersburg with you. It is so long ago since I had the opportunity to taste your lovely soup, sleep on the comfortable couch under the warm eiderdown, listen to the high–pitched laugh of our dear 'Fatty'; in short, to enjoy the charms of life with you of which the most important is to be with you and kiss you as often as possible. . . .

I kiss your hands and embrace dear 'Bun'.

Your son
Piotr

VICTORIAN ENGLAND

1872–1898

QUEEN VICTORIA
1819–1901

Victoria became Queen in 1837. She must have written dozens of letters a day, mostly official, but she still found time to write to her children. These letters to her eldest daughter, Vicky, cover a whole range of subjects and are extremely lively, personal and often heavily underlined to emphasize a point. They illustrate a side of Queen Victoria which is often unrecognized. On the one hand she shows her close devotion as a mother and grandmother, discussing in detail her theories and experiences on child-rearing and the suitability of future husbands and wives. On the other hand she sometimes abandons official discretion and says exactly what she thinks about her ministers. Her love for Disraeli is undisguised. Here she writes to her daughter, the Crown Princess of Prussia.

Buckingham Palace
May 8, 1872

Darling Child,

I am most thankful to hear you are going on so satisfactorily. I never thought you cared (having 3 of each) whether it was a son or daughter; indeed I think many Princes a great misfortune – for they are in one another's and almost everybody's way. I am sure it is the case here – and dear Papa felt this so much that he was always talking of establishing if possible one or two of your brothers and eventual grandchildren (of which I fear there is the prospect of a legion with but little money) in the colonies. I don't dislike babies, though I think very young ones rather disgusting, and I take interest in those of my children when they are two or three – and of people who are dear to me and whom I am fond of – but when they come at the rate of three a year it becomes a cause of mere anxiety for my own children and of no great interest. What name is this fourth daughter to have?....

Windsor Castle
26 June 1872

I have been this morning (driving round) to the Agricultural Show of the Counties of Hampshire and Berkshire held in the Home Park where the one in '51 was held. It is very prettily arranged and there are some very fine beasts.

I come now to this very important subject of the position of the working classes. You know that I have a very strong feeling on that subject. I think the conduct of the higher classes of the present day very alarming – for it is amusement and frivolity from morning till night – which engenders selfishness, and there is a toleration of every sort of vice with impunity in them. Whereas the poorer and working classes who have far less education and are much more exposed – are abused for the tenth part less evil than their betters commit without the slightest blame. The so called immorality of the lower classes is not to be named on the same day with that of the higher and highest. This is a thing which makes my blood boil, and they will pay for it.

Then as regards education – I quite agree with you that it should be enlightened and that the Protestants may not in Germany at least be as earnest as the R. Catholics. But while no one abhors intolerance or spiritual despotism more than I do – no one also has a greater horror than I have of attempts to teach doubts in God's and our Saviours's love and mercy and power, or in His all pervading influence. Teach them to doubt these – and you at once destroy their respect for and faith in anything and that is one of the causes of Communism, for the respect for God and religion goes hand in hand with the respect for authority and law.

These two points I consider are the great dangers and cause Communism. The Jesuits are a fearful body – and I am doubtful whether any laws can be severe enough against them. But I really do not know the state of the case abroad sufficiently well; still I know dear Papa always thought they should be turned out of any country. The case of the women is one which I have a very strong feeling upon. I think they should be sensibly educated – and employed whenever they can be usefully, but on no account unsexed and made doctors (except in one branch), lawyers, voters etc. Do that, and you take at once away all their claim to protection on the part of the male sex. I have not written this well for I have been sadly interrupted but I hope to explain myself better when I have more time. Could you let me have it back to get it copied?

From the Crown Princess to her mother, the Queen, bewailing the fact that she feels slightly out of control where the courtship of her daughter is concerned.

Pavillon D'Ostende
21 July 1877

How differently the younger generation expects to be treated from what we were. Fancy Charlotte never tells me when she writes to Bernard or when he writes to her – they correspond daily almost, I believe, but he would be quite furious if I were only to ask, and she consider herself highly offended and very indignant if her letters were interfered with. Fritz thinks this all right for a German engaged couple and says it ought to be so, but considering how young and how immature she is, I have my little doubts sometimes, and find it rather difficult to know what to do. They resent the slightest restraint put upon them and Bernard thinks they ought to do just as they like – so I am obliged to let it all alone. I am sure you would not have allowed me half so much independence as they get, and I think I was not so queer as Charlotte is; but however young people will be very headstrong and one cannot keep one's influence if one stands too much on one's authority and in Germany certainly the ideas are different.

The Queen's inevitable reply:

Osborne
25 July 1877

. . . . I cannot help smiling at your complaints about Charlotte, I – and dear Papa even if possible more than me – so very much disapproved of that system of complete intimacy before marriage, and in that respect I am bound to say that you never gave us the slightest trouble or annoyance, but Fritz did, and made me very impatient. You were in other ways very difficult to manage, but not in that. I think there is a great want of propriety and delicacy as well as dutifulness in at once treating your bridegroom as though (except in one point) he were your husband. Papa felt this so strongly and it applies still more strongly to very long engagements like yours, your sisters' and Charlotte's. You, as time goes on, I am sure will change your great passion for marriage – and will understand the great change it is to a mother especially, though to a father too! Here now they have lost all modesty for not only do they go about driving, walking, and visiting – everywhere alone, they have also now taken to go out everywhere together in society – which till a year or so no young lady just engaged, ever did, and make a regular show of themselves – and are laughed at and stared at! In short young people are getting very American, I fear in their views and ways.

Balmoral Castle,
22 September 1878

The prospect of your becoming a grandmother and I a great–grandmother might no doubt have been advantageously delayed but I am half–pleased at it. But you need never fear my telling the Empress anything concerning your children or families in the way of news. I never do that.

Osborne
11 August 1880

And now let me say how horrified and how distressed I am about your cat! It is monstrous – and the man ought to be hung on the tree. I could cry with you as I adore my pets. When they belonged to a loved and lost object it must be quite a grief! We always put a collar with V.R. on our pet cats and that pre-serves them. Our keeper once shot a pet one of Beatrice's. Keepers are very stupid but none would dream of mutilation of an animal here! I think it right and only due to the affection of dumb animals, who (the very intelligent and highly developed ones) I believe to have souls to mourn for them truly and deeply.

With Prince Albert's early death, Queen Victoria had to bear the burden of monarchy alone, but later she would confide to her daughter some of her private opinions on matters of state. In this letter the Queen reveals her feelings on her new Liberal Government of 1880. The Queen's opinion of her new Prime Minister, Gladstone, is very dif-ferent from her opinion of the outgoing Disraeli.

Windsor Castle
2 May 1880

I am very tired and have so much to do. Tomorrow is another Council. I send you here a list of the Government. All these Radicals are a great trial – but they may not prove dangerous when in office. Still it alarms people. The first council was a great trial. To take people I cannot trust and whose object was to drive the late Government, which had done so well, out merely to put themselves in, and who will have to pursue much the same policy or there will be war and every sort of disaster – is dreadful – is a dreadful trial. To me "the people's William" is a most disagreeable person – half crazy, and so excited – (though he has been respectful and proper in his manner and professes devotion) to have to deal with. I insisted on receiving assurances on the subject of the principles and languages of Mr. Chamberlain and especially Sir C. Dilke. The last named has made confessions of sins, and promises not to repeat them. He is only an Under Secretary.

The great principle of the Conservative Party is to be for the Throne and Country and of the Liberals "the Party". This is just the difference which now for long I have experienced.

I also send you dear Lord Beaconsfield's letter to me so beautifully and touchingly expressed.

I also send you a very pretty article on Lily's marriage. As we know no morganatic marriage in England I shall announce it just as I did Ernest of Hanover's and Louise's.

OSCAR WILDE
1854–1900

Oscar Wilde studied at Trinity College Dublin and then at Magdalen College Oxford before embarking on his turbulent career as playwright, novelist, wit and aesthete. His character is evident even at the age of 13 when he wrote this letter to his mother, with whom he was on excellent terms. It was written from his school, Portora Royal, in Enniskillen.

Portora School
September 1868

Darling Mama,

The hamper came today, and I never got such a jolly surprise, many thanks for it, it was more than kind of you to think of it. Don't please forget to send me the *National Review* ....The flannel shirts you sent in the hamper are both Willie's, mine are one quite scarlet and the other lilac but it is too hot to wear them yet. You never told me anything about the publisher in Glasgow, what does he say? And have you written to Aunt Warren on the green note paper?

MARQUESS OF QUEENSBURY
1844-1900

Lord Alfred Douglas's association with Oscar Wilde caused widespread scandal and the Marquess of Queensberry, Alfred's father, was determined to stop the relationship and bring Wilde to ruin. This is a letter from Queensberry to his son, written shortly after they met at the Café Royal.

Carter's Hotel,
Albemarle Street,
1 April 1894

Alfred,

It is extremely painful for me to have to write to you in the strain I must; but please understand that I decline to receive any answers from you in writing in return. After your recent hysterical impertinent ones I refuse to be annoyed with such, and I decline to read any more letters. If you have anything to say do come here and say it in person. Firstly, am I to understand that, having left Oxford as you did, with discredit to yourself, the reasons of which were fully explained to me by your tutor, you now intend to leaf and loll about and do nothing. All the time you were wasting at Oxford I was put off with the assurance that you were eventually to go into the Civil Service or to the Foreign Office, and then I was put off with an assurance that you were going to the Bar. It appears to me that you intend to do nothing. I utterly decline, however, to just supply you with sufficient funds to enable you to leaf about. You are preparing a wretched future for yourself, and it would be most cruel and wrong for me to encourage you in this. Secondly, I come to the more painful part of this letter – your intimacy with this man Wilde. It must either cease or I will disown you and stop all money suppplies. I am not going to try and analyse this intimacy, and I make no charge; but to my mind to pose as a thing is as bad as to be it. With my own eyes I saw you both in the most loathsome and disgusting relationship as expressed by your manner and expression. Never in my experience have I ever seen such a sight as that in your horrible features. No wonder people are talking as they are. Also I now hear on good authority, but this may be false, that his wife is petitioning to divorce him for sodomy and other crimes. Is this true, or do you know of it? If I thought the actual thing was true, and it became public property, I should be quite justified in shooting him at sight. These Christian English cowards and men, as they call themselves, want waking up.

Your disgusted so-called father,

Queensberry

Bosie's response to this letter was to send his father a telegram which read: "What a funny little man you are! Alfred Douglas." Queensberry rose to this:

You impertinent young jackanapes. I request that you will not send such messages to me by telegraph. If you send me any more such telegrams, or come with any impertinance, I will give you the thrashing you deserve. Your only excuse is that you must be crazy. I hear from a man at Oxford that you were thought crazy there, and that accounts for a good deal that has happened. If I catch you again with that man I will make a public scandal in a way you little dream of; it is already a suppressed one. I prefer an open one, and at any rate I shall not be blamed for allowing such a state of things to go on. Unless this acquaintance ceases I shall carry out my threat and stop all supplies, and if you are not going to make any attempt to do something I shall certainly cut you down to a mere pittance, so you know what to expect.

A.A. MILNE
1882–1956

Though Alan Alexander Milne wrote plays, novels, poetry, short stories and essays they were overshadowed by his one great creation – Winnie the Pooh – which he wrote for his son, Christopher Robin.

Towards the end of his life, he said of the following letter, "This must have been the first letter which I ever wrote. It was written at the age of four from my kindergarten school. I never did like collaboration, and it is clear that I spurned it on this occasion. All around me (I like to think) were other little boys and girls writing to their dear mammas; asking their companions how to spell Hampstead Heath, or waiting glassy-eyed for some suggestion from the mistress as to what constituted 'a letter'. I just sailed ahead, tongue out, arms outspread. We had had a sanambil, and I had decided to be a carpenter. The family would expect to be told. If anybody else has ever had a sanambil, I should like him to get in touch with me. The word is clearly written, the 'bil' heavily inked over; as if I had played with the idea of some other ending, but realized in time that this combination of letters was the most informative. Could I have meant a 'scramble'? One from whose pen "piggy-backs" flowed so faultlessly would surely have made a better beginning of it. Well, we shall never know now; but I like to think of it as one of those pleasant Victorian games, now gone with so much else of those days which was good."

96 Boundary Road
20 Nov 1886

My dear Mama

We went to Hamstid Heft yestoday. We had a sanambil. We had piggybacks.

I want sme tools ples Mama
lost of OOOOOOO O O OOO
OOO OO O OOOOO OO O OOOOOOOO OO OO OO
You loving
Alan

And a month later:

Dec 15th 1886

My dear Mama.

We are not going to have any more lessons after Tuesday Dr Gibson is coming to give away the prizes. We are to come at a quarter to four on Wednesday and I think I shall have a prize.

With love and kisses.

Your loving

Alan.

WINSTON CHURCHILL
1874 –1965

Winston Churchill was born in Blenheim Palace, Oxfordshire, the elder of two sons of Lord Randolph Churchill. The young Winston Churchill was a chunky lad with a mop of red hair who suffered an unhappy childhood. He spoke with a stutter and lisp and his stubbornness and high spirits annoyed everyone. His parents were too busy to have much time for him. Later he wrote of his mother, Jennie, Lady Randolph Churchill, 'She shone for me like the Evening Star. I loved her dearly – but at a distance.'

He started school at Harrow at the age of 12 and was always bottom of the class but it was there that he began to love the English language, there, he said, that he "got into my bones the essential structure of the ordinary English sentence—"

In this letter written whilst away at Harrow, Winston Churchill, aged 14, writes to his mother. His career at Harrow may have been undistinguished but he appears to have a sense of humour and writes a succinct letter.

Dearest Mamma,

I am going to write you a proper epistle, hoping you will forgive my former negligence. On Saturday we had a lecture on the

'Phonograph'

By 'Col Gouraud'. It was very amusing he astonished all sober-minded People by singing into the Phonograph

'John Brown Body lies- Mouldy in the grave

And is soul goes marching on

Glory, glory, glory Halleluja'

And the Phonograph spoke it back in a voice that was clearly audible in the 'Speech Room'

He shewed us it in private on Monday. We went in 3 or 4 at a time.

His boys are at Harrow.

He fought at Gettysburg.

His wife was at school with you.

Papa gave him letter of introduction to India.

He told me to ask Papa if he remembered the 'tall Yankee'.

I want to be allowed to join the Harrow work shop for they then supply you wood and I want to make some scenery for the nursery if we have any Party. 3 or 4 scenes cost about 1/2 a sovereign and the man who is in charge thoroughly understands scenery making.

With love & kisses I remain

Winston S. Churchill

P.S. Will you write to say whether I may join as I have no imployment for odd half hours. W.C.

GILBERT KEITH CHESTERTON
1874–1936

G.K. Chesterton was a writer of essays and novels and particularly well-known for his Father Brown stories featuring a Roman Catholic priest very skilled in detective work. (Chesterton himself was a renowned Catholic). His masterly style in his writing was matched by his larger-than-life character. He could not have been easy to live with owing to his absent mindedness and lack of worldly wisdom. There is a lovely story recalled in Michael Finch's biography of Chesterton: One morning the Chesterton's housemaid heard him get out of the bath followed by a huge splash as he got in again. "Dammit," he shouted, "I've been here before!"

In the summer of 1898 Chesterton made a proposal of marriage to Frances Blogg and was accepted by her, but he was unable to find the courage to tell his parents; he was much dominated by his mother who had already made up her mind that he ought to marry a childhood friend, Annie Fermin. He joined his parents and brother on their summer holidays but finding it impossible to tell them face-to-face, he sat down one evening and wrote them a letter. This he handed to his mother as they said goodnight, with a request to read it in private. He explains in the letter that she might think it "a somewhat eccentric proceeding" but he had a reason "because it occurs to me that you might possibly wish to turn the matter over in your mind before writing or speaking to me about it".

G.K. CHESTERTON TO HIS MOTHER

Suffolk

Summer 1898

Do not be frightened: or suppose that anything sensational or final has occurred. I am not married, my dear mother, neither am I engaged. You are called to the council of chiefs very early in the deliberations. If you don't mind I will tell you, briefly, the whole story.

You are, I think, the shrewdest person for seeing things whom I know: consequently I imagine that you do not think I go down to Bedford Park every Sunday for the sake of the scenery. . . The first half of my acquaintance with the Bloggs was spent in enjoying a very intimate, but quite breezy and Platonic friendship with Frances Blogg, reading, talking and enjoying life together, having great sympathies on all subjects; and the second half in making the thrilling, but painfully responsible discovery that Platonism, on my side, had not the field by any means to itself. . . . I will not say that you are sure to like Frances, for all young men say that to their mothers, quite naturally, and their mothers never believe them, also quite naturally. Besides, I am so confident, that I should like you to find out for yourself. She is, in reality, very much the sort of woman you like, what is called, I believe, "a Woman's Woman", very humorous, inconsequent and sympathetic and defiled with no offensive exuberance of good health. . . . .Here you give me a cup of cocoa. Thank you.

Believe me, my dearest mother, always your very affectionate son,

Gilbert.

His mother's immediate reaction is not known, but she was a woman of strong likes and dislikes and, according to Annie Fermin, always disliked Frances. Nevertheless Gilbert and Frances were married and Frances allowed his genius to flourish by keeping him free from day to day domestic distractions.

THE MODERNISTS

1898–1917

FREDERICK DELIUS
1862–1934

Delius was born of German and Dutch ancestry. His family were wool traders in Bradford and although he showed an early gift for music he met strong parental opposition to his suggestion of music as a career and he began training for the family business. However, his business travels abroad only served to further develop his passion for music. Eventually Grieg persuaded Delius' father to allow Frederick to become a composer. He married in 1897 and settled in France where he remained for the rest of his life.

There follows two letters from Mrs Delius to her son written soon after his move to France; both are preoccupied with the subject of money.

Claremont
December 1900

My dear Fritz!

Thank you for your good wishes for a happy Christmas which I return. It is not like the olden times where your children were all at Home. I asked Papa to let you have again 5£ a month for a time and he said he would. We stopped as you know by your suggestion, when you got that Grove. I would sell or let it. We were only wishful for you not to have too much charged to you. You have had 1269£ allready, and you know all will be charged to everyone. The elder children have 15,000£ allready. Clare has got every penny she will ever get. But enough of this, you know best what to do! . . . .

. . . . I will tell Shaw (secretary to Delius & Co.) to send you 5£ regulary. I am only sorry that we are not rich people or by God I would give you anything. That money from Oncle Theodore dwindled down to very little. We don't know what has become of it.

Now goodbye dear I wish you good luck in your career and remaine

Your loving Mother

Bradford

13 Jany 1900

Dear Fritz!

Your letter, to say the least, astonished me. You say we left you alone just when you require help; that is a simple untruth. Papa has spend more money on you, than he ought to have done. That you went to Virginia was your blessing, as that was the only time you made a living. Then you were send to Leipzig which again cost hundreds, with the intention to make a degree and go back to Amerika to get on better. Instead of that you choose to remain in Paris where for 5 years got 120£ a year. Even Uncle Theodore told us you ought to go back to America.

Then for more years you got 60£ a year and all your travelling expenses paid. Then *you* wrote that, if Papa would send you the deeds of the Grove, you could do whithout more help. Now you want money again, though Uncle left you 1000£ on whose interest you might have lived in some other town.

What you write about lessons is simply nonsense. How about Halle, Bethoven, Mozart, Paderewsky, Rubinstein etz. Where there is a will there is a way. You will have to do something on your future fame you can not live. Go back, as we have told you over and over to America, *there* you have a future, as I know of other musicians.

You speak of your share of Uncle's money, you have no share, as we have consulted a lawyer and he also says that the money is left to mon frere Julius it only mentions 12 parts as he is getting so much more that his sister. She also keeps the money.

Max has *not* gone bad because he could not do as he liked, but because he has been entangled with low people, and did not stick to business. *Every* father he says when a boy is 21 not 36, that he now has to make his own living. Papas fault has been is kindness. Paper never *lost* this money but his children you, Minnie, Rose etz cost too much.

We have always been careful and I dont choose to begin to retrench with the three girls as I am getting old.

So more money for you is quite out of the question. Go to America or remain it is the same to us. We shall be pleased if you become famous and hope so, but *we* have done our share towards it and *nobody* can say that we have not.... You know dear Fritz, it is very sad for me to have to write to you such letters, to you, who has always had so much done for him.

Papa must under no condition be bothered any more, I want him to have piece.

Your loving Mother

JAMES JOYCE
1882–1941

James Joyce, author of *Portrait of an Artist as a Young Man*, *Dubliners*, *Ulysses* and *Finnegans Wake*, was born in Rathgan, Dublin. He attended University College, Dublin and as the eldest, Joyce was expected to stay on in Dublin and provide for the family – something his father was unable to do due to his alcoholism and inability to keep a job. However, in 1902 Joyce went to Paris for a year where he lived in poverty and wrote poetry. It was here that he met the great circle of writers of the modernist era such as Ernest Hemingway, Gertrude Stein, Ezra Pound, as well as artists such as Pablo Picasso and Henri Braque. He returned to Dublin for his mother's death and then left Ireland more or less for good with Nora Barnacle. Together they lived in Trieste, Zurich and finally, after the war, in Paris.

JOHN STANISLAUS JOYCE TO HIS SON JAMES JOYCE (JIM) IN PARIS

Dublin
31 January 1903

My Dear Jim

May I be permitted to offer you my best wishes for your future which I, at one time, fancied may have been more rosey on your attaining your majority but, circumstances alter cases, and as my cases are circumstantial I must ask you to forgive me, Jim, for the 'might have been'. However I hope you will believe me that I am only now, under I may tell you, *very trying times*, endevouring to do my little best, but Jim you are my eldest Son I have always looked up to your being a fitting representative of *our* family one that my father would be proud of. I now hope that you may carry out *his* ideas through your life and if you do, you may be sure you will not do anything unbecoming a gentleman, but that I am pressed for time I should write you more fully but tomorrow, Jim, I will write to you again. Your fond FATHER

JAMES JOYCE TO HIS FATHER

Grand Hotel Corneille
Paris
26 February 1903

Dear Pappie

I received your telegraph order on Tuesday afternoon and dined. As it was the evening of the carnival, I allowed myself some luxuries – a cigar, confetti to throw, and a supper. I bought a stove, a saucepan, a plate, a cup, a saucer, a knife, a fork, a small spoon, a big spoon, a bowl, salt, sugar, figs, macaroni, cocoa & c and got my linen from the laundry. I now try to do my own cooking. For instance last night for dinner I had two hard–boiled eggs (these are sold here hard–boiled during Lent in red shells) bread and butter, macaroni; a few figs and a cup of cocoa. Today for dejeuner I had some cold ham, bread and butter, Swiss cream with sugar; for dinner I had two poached eggs and Vienna bread, macaroni and milk, a cup of cocoa and a few figs. On Sunday for dinner I shall make a mutton stew – mutton, a few potatoes, mushrooms and lentils, with cocoa and biscuits after. Tomorrow (for dejeuner) I shall finish my ham with bread and butter, Swiss cream and sugar, and finish my figs. I think I shall reduce my expenses in this way. Anyhow I hope I shall not fall asleep now as I used dreaming of rice–pudding, which for one who is fasting is not a nice dream. I am sorry to say that after my dinner on Tuesday I became very ill and at night I had ta fit of vomiting, I felt very bad the whole of the following day but I am better today except for attacks of neuralgia – induced, I imagine, by my constant periods of fasting . . . .

The 'miserable mistake' referred to by Jim's father in the following letter is Joyce's elopement with Nora Barnacle. John Joyce knew nothing of his son's relationship with her until the two had left Ireland together.

9 Millmount Terrace, Drumcondra
24 April 1907

Dear Jim,

I wrote Stannie some fourteen days ago and have not since received any reply? although I fully explained our wretched plight here. I am forced to the conclusion that I have entirely faded out of your memories, well, I am now so accustomed to all sorts of unnatural treatment since your Mother died, both from you and those here, I have arrived at last, *I regret to say*, at a determination to follow your example, and too, *try* to forget. I need not tell *you* how your miserable mistake affected my already well crushed feeling, but then maturer thoughts took more the form of pity than anger, when I saw a life of promise crossed and a future that might have been brilliant blasted in one breath. However I will not reproach you, for I feel certain your own inmost soul and heart (if you possess one?) must do that.

You know I did all in my power to forward your every wish, and any money I could by *any means* get I gave you ungrudgingly. So you can well understand *my feelings* when I discovered my dream so ruthlessly dispelled, my hopes – proud hopes – shattered, and alone left to me, to eke out the few remaining years of misery and loneliness, until God will take pity ony wretchedness and end my unhappy life. My excuse for writing this is that it is possibly the last communication you will ever receive from me, for as matters stand at present here a big change is about to take place and I wish to put you in possession of all the facts. So that you may know my future actions are the outcome of circumstances I do not covet and cannot control. In your letter of the 9th Feby. you say 'I have a great horror lest you should think, that now that I have gained some kind of a position for myself, I wish to hear no more of you & on the contrary I assure you, if you will show me what I can do or get others to do I shall do my best to give the ball another kick.' You also ask me 'what is the amount of my pension which I have clear . . . .'

> John Joyce continues by explaining how little he has to live on after paying living expenses and looking after his large family and dog. He is distraught with worry and wracked with bitterness. He wants to get the children off his hands, his son a job and his sister, Poppie, who has looked after the house since his wife died, out of the house.

. . . . At present as you see I have barely enough to support and dress myself, after helping to provide for the 3 young children. As I am to be evicted from her with the next week or so, I am looking for lodgings for myself but must get the little ones fixed first. Now you know all, and see how I am driven to the wall. So that whatever you may hear of me (as no doubt you will, from those highly respectable people, you so constantly correspond with) or wherever I may be, possible Cork, don't you forget that anything or any place must be some relief from the miserable existence I have put over since August 13th, 1903! For the few, very few I sincerely hope, years I have yet to live I'll try if I can find some of my old friends of long ago who may be glad to see me again, and even amongst strangers I may receive respect and perhaps even affection, refused me by my children. Perhaps in years to come, long after my release from this world, you may learn to feel some of the pangs I have endured, and then you will appreciate the feelings of a Father who loved his children and had high ambitions for them, and spared no money when he could afford it, to educate and make them what they should be, but who when adversity came and he could no longer gratify all those wants, was despised disrespected, jeered at, scoffed at and set at defiance . . . .

Goodbye, Jim, and may God protect you, is the prayer of you still fond and loving, though broken hearted,

Father

T. E. LAWRENCE
1888–1933

The First World War dispatched Thomas Edward Lawrence to the Middle East and transformed him into Lawrence of Arabia. His role in the Arab Revolt provided the material for *The Seven Pillars of Wisdom* which has since become one of the outstanding accounts of guerilla warfare. Lawrence was a complex personality – a man of action and of great romanticism, a lover of people and publicity.

In the following letter to his mother, T.E Lawrence, aged 18, already shows his breezy independence of spirit and the practical side of his nature. Arnie is his youngest brother, A.W. Lawrence, and the Mont he refers to is Mont St Michel.

Dinard
Monday, 6th August 1906

. . . . I am rather surprised about the Morris; it should not have broken like that. Tell Arnie I am not coming back for a long time; not for weeks: there are wolves quite close to a part which we will visit on our tour (close means forty miles). It appears that there are a number of mountains about, and the country is quite wild; the wolves did a lot of damage last winter. I cannot promise to kill one for Wil . . . . all this morning I have been wrestling with tyres of Will's old bicycle here, I removed three outer covers (without the one minute removers) took out and exchanged 3 inner tubes; changed two valves, tightened a chain, and adjusted the bearings of a wheel, all in two hours. Please give my kindest regards to Father and the rest and *don't work too hard*: do nothing rather than too much; you are worth more than the house; love to all: hope you are all well: I have not been bilious yet; don't expect to be. A flock of sheep disappeared in the sands round the Mont this spring and so I will not try to find them. Ta Ta. Love. love. love. love. love love. Ned

ALAIN-FOURNIER
1886–1914

Born Henri-Alban Fournier in La Chapelle d'Angillon, France, Alain-Fournier spent most of his childhood in Epineuil, where his father was a country schoolmaster. He attended naval college in Brest but decided against a naval career and studied next in Paris. *Le Grand Meaulnes*, his only novel, was inspired by his childhood and Yvonne Brochet, the woman who haunted him throughout his life. Alain-Fournier disappeared on the Meuse on 22 September 1914, presumed killed in action.

This nostalgic letter was written to his parents from the Lycée de Lakanal in Paris. In it he conjures up the sights and sounds of country life and describes romantically what it meant to him as a child. Fournier had inherited from his mother and his grandmother a deep love of home. He had already decided that he wanted to be a writer.

20 March 1905

. . . . Here (at Lakanal), the large blind of the big window looking out over the vast, depressing suburb, flaps to and fro; from time to time, either across my eyes or on to the corner of this letter, falls a bright beam of sunshine which is almost gay . . . .

And yet I'm just a little sad at heart because all that this sunshine can light up around me here, are the dust–motes stirred up by the dirty, ugly boy beside me, and the dusty set books, always the same.

Because all that the great and glorious sunshine can now light upon is that dry, grey little playground where your pupils are shouting – pupils who aren't the brothers or the children of those who used to stay behind after school to play with me *in the other place;*

– because beneath this same sun, you have only a paltry garden, practically public property, where Mother with her sunshade and Father with his spade can no longer linger for as long as they please, for as long as they used to along the paths of long ago between our strawberry beds, near Old Martin's field, all big and still and silent, beside the stream which used to hide itself away in that field, covered with branches, full of shadows and mystery;

– because nowhere now can this sunshine light on the *things* I love and which belong to me–belong to me to such an extent that they're almost part of me – such as the hawthorn hedges in the garden, full of nettles, garden mint, chervil and sweet–smelling herbs; like the wistaria on the playground shed; like that little wooden door with the squeaking bolt which you'd pull back to find three eggs nestling in the straw.

I don't suppose that any of those things are part of *your* hearts because you'll scarcely even have seen them, because you were already grown–up and caught up in the business of living. But that is where we were just emerging into the world, and all that we've learnt to feel and know about our hearts, about happiness, about sweetness or sorrow, we learnt in the school playground where, on our melancholy Thursdays, all that could be heard was the crowing of cocks from the village, and in my bedroom where, through the fanlight, the sun would shine down on my two statuettes of the Holy Virgin and on the red cushion, and in the classroom where, as Father supervised 'prep', through the open windows would come with the branches of the apple–trees, all the gentle warm sunshine of five o'clock and the full fine fragrance of freshly dug earth.

You simply have to realise that for me, all those things are all the world, and I feel that my heart consists of nothing else . . . . I want to write books and books for you about everything *one* saw and felt in that little corner of the earth which was our whole World – and about the corner in my heart where it goes on living still . . . .

In December 1907 Fournier was singled out for training as a possible officer and although he dreaded being away from Paris he explains the benefits to his parents.

. . . . For my last six months of Army service, I'd be a lieutenant in the Reserve, and the training would make the two years pass much more quickly. And I'd end up with an extra qualification for my career in the Colonies. My mind is still fixed on that. I don't want, after four years of study, to end up as a miserable little school–teacher. I think that these years in the Army, sad though they are, will toughen me up for that final departure. At this moment in time, the very thought of it breaks my heart. But the prospects are great, promotion should be quick, and it'll always be possible to get back again. At the end of my Army service, I thought of taking things easy at home with you for a month or two, then asking if you might finance me for a year in England. Once there, I could really perfect my English conversation, and this would serve me well either if I decided to leave for Indochina or else if I go peacefully on studying for the agregation exam in English and Literature. In the course of that year, I'd be able to make up my mind absolutely clearly and calmly. Wouldn't you like that?. . . .

WOMEN IN EUROPE

1913–1914

ANNA FREUD
1895–1982

Anna Freud was born in Vienna, the youngest of six children of Sigmund Freud and Martha Berneys. Sigmund Freud greatly advanced the thinking in psychiatry with his theories on the effect of the unconscious mind upon behaviour. Anna was profoundly influenced by his work and became a distinguished psychoanalyst in her own right. The family came to London in 1938 to escape the Nazi occupation of Austria – Hitler had banned psychoanalysis in 1933. After Freud's death in 1939 his daughter Anna, who was already contributing to the development of child psychiatry, took up his mantle.

In the following letter Anna, aged 18, replies to her father who had written to calm her and to suggest that she was jealous of Max Halberstadt who was to marry one of Anna's elder sisters; he suggested, in psychoanalytical terms, the wedding had produced in her the negative Oedipal feelings a girl may have when she experiences a brother–in–law or a father as a rival for the love of a sister or mother. This suggestion was greeted with incredulity. Anna was staying in Merano to improve her health and was not to be allowed to return to Vienna for the wedding.

Merano
7 January 1913

Dear Papa,

I got your letter today and wanted to write to you anyway, to thank you for your last letter, which made me very happy. I am now quite well again, and hope that whatever I had will not recur – I wondered a great deal what it was, for I am not really sick. It irrupts in me, somehow, and then I am very tired and must worry about all kinds of things, which at other times are just a matter of course: about my being here, and that I do nothing all day long when I got sick, and similar things. I am no longer embroidering Sophie's tablecloth, and it is unpleasant when I think about that, for I would like to have finished it. Naturally, I think rather often about Sophie's wedding, but I am indifferent about Max, because he is a complete stranger to me; I don't really like him, but I am certainly not jealous of him. It is not nice to say it, but I am glad that Sophie is getting married, because the unending quarrel between us was horrible for me. It was no matter for her, because she did not care for me, but I liked her very much and I always admired her a bit. I cannot, however, understand why she is marrying Max, for she hardly knows him. But I cannot think that his presence in Vienna and all that has any connection with how I feel and I truly do not know why I am sometimes quite well and sometimes not, and I would like very much to know, so that I can do something to help myself. I would like very much to be reasonable like Mathilde, and I don't know why with me everything takes so long. I am really very well, I like it here, and when I come back to Vienna I can start again all the things I like to do. But if I have a stupid day, everything looks wrong to me; for instance, today I cannot understand how it can sometimes be so stupid. I do not want to have it again, for I want to be a reasonable person or at least to become one, but I can't always help myself alone. When I had something like that in Vienna, I always talked to Trude about it and then everything was alright.

Please understand that I would not have written all this to you, because I do not want to worry you, if you had not written as you did. Now I am well and you will see that I will return to Vienna all strong and healthy, because I want it absolutely then it does happen. I weighed myself today and I had gained another half a kilo, and I purposefully went for a long walk, which did not tire me as before. The weather and the sun are more and more beautiful and warm, and I look forward to the time when everything starts blooming – which won't be long here. Walks are much more beautiful here than in Vienna and you would have liked everything very much had you come here, which would have been so lovely. I send you many, many greetings and a kiss and could you please write to me soon again, for I will become more reasonable if you will help me.

Your Anna

P.S. I could not write more to you, because I don't know more myself, but I certainly do not keep any secrets from you.

MARIE CURIE
1867–1934

Manya Sklodovska was born in Poland in 1867 and died a much honoured scientist in Paris in 1934. In November 1891 she went to Paris and entered the Sorbonne to study science. There she used the French version of her name, Marie, on her registration certificate. At the Sorbonne Marie met and fell in love with another scientist of genius, Pierre Curie, eight years her senior. They were married in the summer of 1895. Their first daughter, Irene, was born in the Autumn of 1897, a second daughter, Eve, followed in December 1904. Despite bringing up this young family, Marie decided that she must also continue her scientific career and she and Pierre worked togther in the most spartan of conditions on the nature of radioactivity. For this work, she and Pierre shared the Nobel prize for physics in 1903 with Becquerel. Pierre was tragically killed in 1906 in a street accident in Paris, but Marie continued to combine her devoted family life with her work. Her discovery of radium led to new fields in medicine and the treatment of cancer. Marie was further honoured for this achievement by a second Nobel prize, this time for chemistry, in 1911.

In July 1914 The Curie Institute was completed with Marie as director. Marie had rented a villa in Brittany for the summer, where Irene and Eve stayed with a governess and a cook while Marie completed university business in Paris before joining them.

MARIE CURIE TO HER DAUGHTERS

Paris

1 August 1914

Dear Irene and Eve – Things seem to be getting worse: we expect mobilisation from one minute to the next. I don't know if I shall be able to leave. Don't be afraid; be calm and courageous. If war does not break out, I shall come and join you on Monday. If it does, I shall stay here and send for you as soon as possible. You and I, Irene, will try and make ourselves useful.

Paris

2 August, 1914

My dear daughters, – Mobilisation has begun, and the Germans have entered France without a declaration of war. We shall not be able to communicate with each other easily for some time.

Paris is calm and gives a good impression, in spite of the grief of the farewells.

Paris
6 August 1914

My dear Irene, – I, too want to bring you back here, but it is impossible for the moment. Be patient.

The Germans are crossing Belgium and fighting their way. Brave little Belgium did not allow them to pass without defending itself . . . . All the French are hopeful, and think that the struggle, although it may be hard, will take a good turn.

Poland is partly occupied by the Germans. What will be left of it after their passage? I know nothing about my family.

> Marie, although not a specialist in X–rays realised their value in the treatment of the wounded in the coming carnage. She organised volunteers, located equipment and manufacturers and, with funds from the Union of Women of France, created radiological cars. These were ordinary cars which carried the X–ray equipment and a generator, in effect, mobile X–ray units which could be driven from hospital to hospital. Marie decided that she must also stay in Paris to protect the Curie Institute from plunder by the German army which was rapidly advancing towards Paris. She prepared her daughters for a possible separation.

MARIE TO IRENE

28 August 1914

. . . . They are beginning to face the possibility of a siege of Paris, in which case we might be cut off. If that should happen, endure it with courage, for our personal desires are nothing in comparison with the great struggle that is now underway. You must feel responsible for your sister and take care of her if we should be separated for a longer time than I expected.

29 August 1914

Dear Irene, – You know there is nothing to prove that we shall be cut off, but I wanted to tell you that we must be ready for all sorts of alternatives . . . . Paris is so near the frontier that the Germans might very well approach it. That must not keep us from hoping that the final victory will be for France.

So, courage and confidence! Think of your role as elder sister, which it is time you took seriously.

> 31 August 1914

. . . . I have just received your sweet letter of Saturday, and I wanted so much to kiss you that I almost cried.

Things are not going very well, and we are all heavy–hearted and disturbed in soul. We need great courage, and I hope that we shall not lack it. We must keep our certainty that after the bad days the good times will come again. It is in this hope that I press you to my heart, my beloved daughters.

MARIE TO IRENE

> 6 September 1914

. . . . The theatre of war is changing at the moment: the enemy seems to be going farther away from Paris. We are all hopeful, and we have faith in final success.

. . . . Make young Fernand Chavannes do his problems in physics. If you cannot work for France just now, work for its future. Many people will be gone, alas, after this war, and their places must be taken. Do your mathematics and physics as well as you can.

The German advance was stopped at the Battle of the Marne and Paris was saved. Eve and Irene returned to Paris, Eve to school, Irene to train as a nurse.

The First World War

1914-1918

Most letters written around this period in some way touch on the First
World War. The war caused many separations amongst all age groups.
Here is one written because of the separation forced by mobilisation.

2ND LIEUTENANT J. MACLEOD
3rd Reserve Battalion
The Queen's Own Cameron Highlanders

The Queensgate Hotel,
Inverness.
August 10th

Dear Mother,

I had a very good journey, a very nice fellow from Tonbridge School, who
is in a firm that supplies electric lights to railways, was the only other occupant
of the compartment, though otherwise the train was crowded. On reaching
Inverness, he took me to his hotel for a shave and wash–up. In this hotel I am
now staying: it is clean, and very moderate – a temperance affair; it gives you
high tea in the evening and no dinner. I never shaved so badly in my life, and
got cut in five places. This was because the blades that I bought at Boots just
do not fit. In spite of wounds I went to the Camerons' place. At first they were
rather brutal, thinking me to be a German spy, I suppose, on account of my
scarred face. They asked me a lot of questions to test my identity. Fortunately
there was another old Rugbeian applying for a similar job. (I had met him
before this painful interview in the Medical Officer's place, whither I was sent
on arrival.) They turned me out of the room and sent for him, interviewing
him separately. The result was that they suddenly turned friendly, and said that
it was all right, but

(i) I would have to wait until I was gazetted, and as there was a rush on the
Regiment, I might be gazetted to some other regiment, and therefore they
would not tell me what kit to get;

(ii)I could not get any kit in Inverness; Edinburgh was the nearest place. They advised me to go back to Cambridge, but that would be fearfully expensive, and cost about an extra £5. So I am going to write to the James' and ask them if they will put me up. I will let you know by wire where I am.

All love,

Jock

Two years later, writing to his father, Jock Macleod has grown up; no longer the mock dramatic tales of pretend war – scarring by shaving and German spies – but a coded message which says, "In train for Marseilles".

Dear Father,

Thank you for your letter. The weather has now turned slightly warmer. We appreciated the change this morning, for we had Reveille at 3.30, breakfast at 4 and started off on a 10 mile march at 5 o'clock.

I am now using a new pony.
Nothing seems to do any good
To my old pony, which still
Remains lame in spite of
All bandages. The pony that
I now have belonged to our origi-
Nal padre, who has left us
For the Base Camp at Havre.
On the completion of his year he
Returns to his parish. He had
Merely six weeks to do until then,
And so the authorities decided to
Retain him in France. It did not
Seem worthwhile to
Employ him with us, and then
Immediately send him back.
Last night we had a
Long rumour that a Bulgarian gen–
Eral had been assassinated.
Sorry that I have no news!
Yours Aye, Jock.

It was difficult for families at home to imagine the appalling conditions of trench warfare on the Western Front, with constant danger and terrible living conditions. It was necessary for the recipient to read between the lines as many soldiers under-played the danger that they were in. In the following letter Major Stubbs, writing from from Ypres Salient makes a joke of his situation which only serves to accentuate the full horror of the war.

MAJOR T.D.H STUBBS
Royal Artillery

My dear little Katherine

Many thanks for your nice letter which I received yesterday. It was good of you to write such a nice letter & in such good writing. I gave your love to Capt. Hedley & Mr. Burnley, but Mr. Ingham & Mr. Harris were both jealous. We live here more like rabbits than anything else & we have a lookout rabbit with glasses & a whistle who blows 3 blasts when he sees a German aeroplane then we all dive below & remain there until our lookout blows one blast. The German aeroplanes have a horrid habit of coming out just as our dinner & tea is being brought up to the Battery with the result that the men carrying the meals have to squat down perhaps 100 yards away. We sit in our rabbit holes & peep out at our dinners while the dinners get cold. It is very annoying of them & is altogether a bad habit but three days ago our airmen went up after one of the Germans & shot him down, he also did the same thing with another the day before yesterday so that is two less anyway to bother us.

I am very well indeed & really am liking the life, if only we don't get too many shells at us. I am sending you a small piece of a shell which came to call yesterday. We were sitting having tea when we heard him & two friends coming, they whistle as they come to show how cheerful they are, this particular one sailed over just beyond the end of the Battery & burst right in the middle of the road 200 yards or so behind. There was a French ambulance coming along the road at the time, the shell must have missed it by inches as it burst only 10 yards behind it, the horse took no notice at all, a Frenchman had the top of his finger blown off & the French surgeon some distance away got it in the leg. One of the other shells burst quite close to another battery but hurt no one.

I went out afterwards & found this piece of shell which you should keep as a souvenir. Some day I will tell you the name of the place. The only other damage done was a blackbird killed which one of our men found & the road with a big hole in it, which we repaired as our wagons use it. We are ordering things for the men to be sent out weekly from Fortnum & Mason so except for a slab or two of chocolate & occasionally a cake I really don't want anything at present. I could do with another dozen drawing pins. We are now getting enough to eat if only the horrid German aeroplanes will leave us alone to eat it. You see it is very important that the German aeroplanes should not be able to see where we are as if they do they will quickly begin to shell us out & we would then have the bother of finding another position & digging our rabbit holes again & of planting a new plantation round the grass, so we are very careful. I have to preside at a Court Martial tomorrow which I am not looking forward to at all. Give my best love to Mummy & heaps to yourself. I know you will be good & will make Mummy happy.

Your own

Daddy

RIFLEMAN B.F. ECCLES

7th (S) Battalion, The Rifle Brigade

France

Monday 16 April 1917

My very dear Mother,

I am quite safe and well. I will not say 'in the pink' as I am feeling just a trifle 'war–worn' but a few days rest will soon make me fit again.

I dare say you have guessed from my last letter and the ensuing week's silence that something was on, and now you will have seen the papers. We have been right there. What a Bank Holiday and Easter week! Somehow or other Bank Holidays seem to be big days with us. It has been a rougher do than the Somme although casualties have not been so heavy. It is the blinking weather! Heavy snowstorms on an open battlefield are no 'cop' especially when one is living for four or five days on 'bully and biscuits'. Water was practically napoo so that thirst was an extra addition to our little troubles.

But there again the saying still holds good 'It is an ill wind' etc, for the snow was a godsend to parched throats. Goodness knows how much I ate that night. We were very lucky again, all my pals being safe. We lost one of our team just as we went over the barbed wire but we are still hoping he may turn up. I think I will say, no battalion could have advanced under a Hellish machine–gun fire with such coolness. The way we went forward was as if on parade.

Now, I am thankful to say I went through it quite well. Although I say it myself I kept cool all the time, and was never once troubled with nerves.

This is a great blessing when under fire for one sees cases of fright. And again Mother dear, I must thank you and Dad for your prayers for I believe a fellow has more than luck on his side to win through.

We are now behind the line for a few days. We reached billets after marching all night on top of days without sleep. Our appearance was not exactly civilised! Sunday to Friday without a wash or shave, and all the time in mud holes etc.

So, my dear Mother, just imagine my joy, on arriving at the billet for there awaiting me was a parcel and four or five days letters. So I had a feed, then rolled up in my blankets and slept from 5 a.m. to 3.30p.m.

We then rose, washed, scraped off the thickest mud, had a meal and went to bed again till next morning. Talk about sleeping like a log. But I did not forget to send up a prayer of thanksgiving to God for my safety.

You will remember I told you I was able to attend Holy Communion twice before going up.

Thanks so much for the five–franc note. Since coming down here I have had many cups of coffee. This morning Milner and I bought a couple of fresh eggs each, and we took them to a French woman I know, and she boiled them for us 'Tres Bon'.

Now Mother Dearest, I must close. Tell the 'ginger kid' I have got a nice little souvenir of the 'big push' which I want him to hang on my bedroom wall. I am endeavouring to get it through by post.

You will see the owner's name on it. He no longer lives.

Well, goodbye for the present. I shall write again soon. Keep cheerful and smiling, and accept the love of

Your very devoted son,
Burton.

ROBERT BRIFFAULT

Briffault was born and brought up in Europe but emigrated to New
Zealand, where he trained as a doctor. He had settled comfortably in a
quiet career when the outbreak of the First World War filled him, as it
did so many others, with the conviction that he must fight not only out
of patriotism, but also to preserve the values of civilisation. The horrors
he experienced prompted doubts in Briffault's mind and he went on to
write a series of philosophical and anthropological works, questioning
the basis and course of western civilisation, which were influential in
the 20's and 30's.

His narrative powers are already evident in this account of the battle
of Passchendaele which he sent to his daughter, Muriel. He later incor-
porated this description of 'the most ghastly night I have ever spent'
into his second novel "Europa in Limbo."

October 1917

. . . . under railway sleepers outside – a kind of lean-to we had built up; one
shell hit it sideways and wounded my servant in the neck. They all had to be
got in inside as best possible. We were seven in all. Two hours later a terrific
crash took place, our candle went out and there were terrified screams. A shell
had landed exactly at the door of the rat-hole and blown right inside. When I
had brushed the mud and muck off my face and told every one to keep perfectly still, I got my flash-light out of my pocket and amid the mass of writhing
and groaning humanity ascertained that my Sergeant (who has been my right
hand for close on a year) was hit through the body, and a corporal had a com-
pound fracture of the thigh. Another man was killed outright. You may - or
rather you cannot, imagine the job it was to dress the two wounded men in
such a hole. We had to get them on to the planks that served as ledges and
performed feats of contortion on the tops of Petrol tins! That night was
beyond comparison the most ghastly night I have ever spent. Cramped in the
most back and limb breaking position between two wounded men who were
calling constantly on me to hold their hand or give them a pull out of my
water bottle, in the impossibility to move a single inch, holding a candle in
one hand - as there was no other place to put it, breathing a pestilential
atmosphere that turned one's stomach - nothing was wanting to complete the
horror of hell. And the shells came dropping again, again on our heads and we

wondered how long the roof would hold out. I looked at my watch and followed the slow creeping of the hours – 1, 2, 3, 4, 5 – at last came 6 o/c and dawn. At that hour the Boche having made sure that no new attack was coming usually slowed down his shelling for an hour or two -it was the breathing-time of the day. We managed after infinite labour to dig ourselves out of the choked entrance, to drag the wounded men out and to carry them to the Advanced Dressing Station . . . .

WILFRED OWEN
1893–1918

Most of the poems for which Wilfrid Owen is remembered were written between the summer of 1917 and the autumn of the following year when he died in action. It was in these poems and those of the other "war poets" that the reality of the war was most vividly expressed.

Having served in the trenches from January to June 1917 he was invalided home. His nerves were shattered and he was sent to Craiglockhart, a military hospital, where he met another poet Siegfried Sassoon. On New Year's Eve, shortly before he returned to the front, he wrote to his mother.

Scarborough
31 December 1917

My own dear Mother,

. . . . Last year, at this time, (it is just midnight, and now is the intolerable instant of the Change) last year I lay awake in a windy tent in the middle of a vast, dreadful encampment. It seemed neither France nor England, but a kind of paddock where the beasts are kept a few days before the shambles . . . .

But chiefly I thought of the very strange look on all faces in that camp; an incomprehensible look, which a man will never see in England . . . .

It was not despair, or terror, it was more terrible than terror, for it was a blindfold look, and without expression, like a dead rabbit's.

It will never be painted, and no actor will ever seize it. And to describe it, I think I must go back and be with them.

We are sending seven officers straight out tomorrow.

I have not said what I am thinking this night, but next December I will surely do so.

I know what you are thinking, and you know me
Wilfrid.

Ten months later.

Thurs. 31 October, 6.15 p.m.

Dearest Mother,

I will call the place from which I'm now writing "The Smoky Cellar of the Forester's House". I write on the first sheet of the writing pad which came in the parcel yesterday. Luckily the parcel was small, as it reached me just before we moved off to the line. Thus only the paraffin was unwelcome in my pack. My servant & I ate the chocolate in the cold middle of last night, crouched under a draughty Tamboo, roofed with planks. I husband the Malted Milk for tonight, & tomorrow night. The handkerchief & socks are most opportune, as the ground is marshy, & I have a slight cold!

So thick is the smoke in this cellar that I can hardly see by a candle 12 ins. away, and so thick are the inmates that I can hardly write for pokes, nudges & jolts. On my left the Coy. Commander snores on a bench; other officers repose on wire beds behind me. At my right hand, Kellett, a delightful servant of A Coy. in *The Old Days* radiates joy & contentment from pink cheeks and baby eyes. He laughs with a signaller, to whose left ear is glued the Receiver; but whose eyes rolling with gaity shows that he is listening with his right ear to a merry corporal, who appears at this distance away (some three feet) nothing [but] a gleam of white teeth & a wheeze of jokes.

Splashing my hand, an old soldier with a walrus moustache peels & drops potatoes into the pot. By him, Keyes, my cook, chops wood; another feeds the smoke with the damp wood.

It is a great life. I am more oblivious than alas! yourself, dear Mother, of the ghastly glimmering of the guns outside, & the hollow crashing of the shells.

There is no danger down here, or if any, it will be well over before you read these lines.

I hope you are as warm as I am; as serene in your room as I am here; and that you think of me never in bed as resignedly as I think of you always in bed. Of this I am certain you could not be visited by a band of friends half so fine as surround me here.

Ever Wilfrid X

This is Owen's last letter; he was killed four days afterwards while crossing the Sambre Canal. The war ended a week later. In October 1918 he was awarded the Military Cross for exceptional bravery in the field.

SERGEANT PHELPS HARDING
306th Infantry Regiment
77th Division
American Expeditionary Force

In March 1918 the Americans sent reinforcements across the Atlantic. This is a letter from one of the American soldiers to his father on the eve of embarkation.

Camp Upton, N.Y.
29 March 1918

Dear Dad,

I just wrote Mother that the regiment is almost ready to leave for France – in fact, it is liable to go any day. I thought it better to tell her a little ahead than to write hurriedly at the last minute, although I know that the news will be quite a blow. Her letter is going the same mail as this.

This letter is addressed to you at the Vermont for strategic reasons– to avoid Mother seeing it. I simply want to tell you that we were secretly, several weeks ago, practically given our preference as to whether we would rather serve here or abroad. That's what I came into the fight for, and I want to see it through. Don't tell Mother that I had an opportunity to stay here, for I know that it would make her feel badly that I did not stay. I am just telling you so that if anything should happen to me you will know that I met the danger of my own free will, and with a full knowledge of what to expect in the fighting on the other side. I'm mighty glad I have the chance to go over and do my share – and I know you are glad to have me go.

As I said before, we are just about ready to leave, and it is rumoured that we will sail before the week ends. My recommendation for a commission has been made, and it is just a question of red tape and a need of officers before I get my 2nd Lieutenancy. That is the only rank given out of this camp. Considering the number of older men and non–commissioned officers in the school, I believe I have done fairly well, for I stand pretty high on the official list, although I do not know the exact number.

Now I'll close. I'll write you again before we leave, even if I have to leave a card here for one of the other men to send.

Lots of love,

Phelps.

TWO AMERICAN NOVELISTS

1907–1944

SCOTT FITZGERALD
1896–1940

Tales of the Jazz Age, The Great Gatsby, Tender is the Night and *The Last Tycoon* made Scott Fitzgerald the leading American novelist of his generaton.

In the following letter to his mother, Scott, aged 10 writes from summer camp.

Camp Chatham
Orillia, Ontario
18 July 1907

Dear Mother,

I received your letter this morning and though I would like very much to have you up here I don't think you would like it as you know no one here except Mrs. Upton and she is busy most of the time. I don't think you would like the accommodations as it is only a small town and no good hotels. There are some very nice boarding houses but about the only fare is lamb and beef. Please send me a dollar because there are a lot of little odds and ends I need. I will spend it cautiously. All the other boys have pocket money besides their regular allowance.

Your loving son,
Scott Fitzgerald

The next letter was written to his mother when he received his commission in the middle of the First World War.

University Cottage Club
Princeton, New Jersey
14 November 1917

Dear Mother;

You were doubtless surprised to get my letter but I certainly was delighted to get my commission.

My pay started the day I signed the Oath of Allegiance and sent it back which was yesterday– Went up to Brooks Brothers yesterday afternoon and ordered some of my equipment.

I haven't received any orders yet but I think I will be ordered to Fort Leaven worth within a month – I'll be there three months and would have six additional months' training in France before I was ordered with my regiment to the trenches.

I get 141 dollars a month (1700 dollars a year) with a 10% increase when I'm in France.

My uniforms are going to cost quite a bit so if you haven't sent me what you have *of my own money please* do so.

I'm continuing here going to classes until I get orders. I am Second Lieutenant in the *regular* infantry and not a reserve officer – I rank with a West Point graduate.

. . . . About the army, please let's not have either tragedy or Heroics because they are equally distasteful to me. I went into this perfectly cold–bloodedly and don't sympathize with the

"Give my son to country" etc

   etc

   etc

or

"Hero stuff"

because I just went and purely for social reasons. If you want to pray, pray for my soul and that I won't get killed – the last doesn't seem to matter particularly and if you are a good Catholic the first ought to.

To a profound pessimist about life, being in danger is not depressing. I have never been more cheerful. Please be nice and respect my wishes.

Love
Scott

In 1920, after the publication of *This Side of Paradise*, which brought
Scott Fitzgerald instant fame, he married Zelda Sayre. She too was a
writer and together they lived a glamorous, fast–moving life, full of
parties, high society and extravagance. They had one daughter, Frances
(Pie).

SCOTT FITZGERALD TO HIS DAUGHTER AGED 12.

La Paix, Rodgers' Forge
Towson, Maryland
8 August 1933

Dear Pie:

I feel very strongly about you doing your duty. Would you give me a little
more documentation about your reading in French? I am glad you are happy –
but I never believe much in happiness. I never believe in misery either. Those
are things you see on the stage or the screen or the printed page, they never
really happen to you in life.

All I believe in in life is the rewards for virtue (according to your talents)
and the *punishments* for not fulfilling your duties, which are doubly costly. If
there is such a volume in the camp library, will you ask Mrs. Tyson to let you
look up a sonnet of Shakespeare's in which the line occurs "Lilies that fester
smell far worse than weeds."

Have had no thoughts today, life seems composed of getting up a *Saturday
Evening Post* story. I think of you, and always pleasantly; but if you call me
"Pappy" again I am going to take the White Cat out and beat his bottom *hard,
six times for every time you are impertinent*. Do you react to that?

I will arrange the camp bill.

Halfwit, I will conclude.

Things to worry about:
Worry about courage
Worry about cleanliness
Worry about efficiency
Worry about horsemanship
Worry about——

Things not to worry about:
Don't worry about popular opinion
Don't worry about dolls
Don't worry about the past
Don't worry about the future
Don't worry about growing up
Don't worry about anybody getting ahead of you
Don't worry about triumph
Don't worry about failure unless it comes through your own fault
Don't worry about mosquitoes
Don't worry about flies
Don't worry about insects in general
Don't worry about parents
Don't worry about boys
Don't worry about disappointments
Don't worry about pleasures
Don't worry about satisfactions

Things to think about:
What am I really aiming at?
How good am I really in comparison to my contemporaries in regard to:
(a) Scholarship
(b) Do I really understand about people and am I able to get along with them?
(c) Am I trying to make my body a useful instrument or am I neglecting it?
With dearest love,
(Daddy)

P.S. My come–back to your calling me Pappy is christening you by the word Egg, which implies that you belong to a very rudimentary state of life and that I could break you up and crack you open at my will and I think it would be a word that would hang on if I ever told it to your contemporaries. "Egg Fitzgerald." How would you like that to go through life with –"Eggie Fitzgerald" or "Bad Egg Fitzgerald" or any form that might occur to fertile minds? Try it once more and I swear to God I will hang it on you and it will be up to you to shake it off. Why borrow trouble?

Love anyhow.

As an only child, Frances Scott (Scottie) was much loved but she had a difficult upbringing. Her mother, Zelda, was very unstable, behaving like another child most of the time and some years before this letter was written she suffered a mental breakdown. The effect of their violent life together had a traumatic affect on Scott, accelerating his drinking.

Here is a heartbreakingly passionate and disappointed letter from father to daughter, in which he gives vent to all his deep–seated worries and frustrations about how his daughter has turned out. However, one can detect the sound of deep love for his child with perhaps a touch of guilt and anguish that he hadn't made it better for her. The rhythm and crescendos of the letter contribute to making it a very powerful piece of writing. Scottie, at this time was aged 17.

(Metro–Goldwyn–Mayer Corporation)
(Culver City, California)
7 July 1938

Dearest Scottie:

I don't think I will be writing letters many more years and I wish you would read this letter twice–bitter as it may seem. You will reject it now, but at a later period some of it may come back to you as truth. When I'm talking to you, you think of me as an older person, an "authority," and when I speak of my own youth what I say becomes unreal to you–for the young can't believe in the youth of their fathers. But perhaps this little bit will be understandable if I put in in writing.

When I was your age I lived with a great dream. The dream grew and I learned how to speak of it and make people listen. Then the dream divided one day when I decided to marry your mother after all, even though I knew she was spoiled and meant no good to me. I was sorry immediately I had married her but, being patient in those days, made the best of it and got to love her in another way. You came along and for a long time we made quite a lot of happiness out of our lives. But I was a man divided – she wanted me to work too much for her and not enough for my dream. She realized too late that work was dignity, and the only dignity, and tried to atone for it by working herself, but it was too late and she broke and is broken forever.

It was too late also for me to recoup the damage – I had spent most of my resources, spiritual and material, on her, but I struggled on for five years till my health collapsed, and all I cared about was drink and forgetting.

The mistake I made was in marrying her. We belonged to different worlds

– she might have been happy with a kind simple man in a southern garden. She didn't have the strength for the big stage – sometimes she pretended, and pretended beautifully, but she didn't have it. She was soft when she should have been hard, and hard when she should have been yielding. She never knew how to use her energy – she's passed that failing on to you.

For a long time I hated *her* mother for giving her nothing in the line of good habit – nothing but "getting by" and conceit. I never wanted to see again in this world women who were brought up as idlers. And one of my chief desires in life was to keep you from being that kind of person, one who brings ruin to themselves and others. When you began to show disturbing signs at about fourteen, I comforted myself with the idea that you were too precocious socially and a strict school would fix things. But sometimes I think that idlers seem to be a special class for whom nothing can be planned, plead as one will with them – their only contribution to the human family is to warm a seat at the common table.

My reforming days are over, and if you are that way I don't want to change you. But I don't want to be upset by idlers inside my family or out. I want my energies and my earnings for people who talk my language.

I have begun to fear that you don't. You don't realize that what I am doing here is the last tired effort of a man who once did something finer and better. There is not enough energy, or call it money, to carry anyone who is dead weight and I am angry and resentful in my soul when I feel that I am doing this. People like . . . . and your mother must be carried because their illness makes them useless. But it is a different story that you have spent two years doing no useful work at all, improving neither your body nor your mind, but only writing reams and reams of dreary letters to dreary people, with no possible object except obtaining invitations which you could not accept. Those letters go on, even in our sleep, so that I know your whole trip now is one long waiting for the post. It is like an old gossip who cannot still her tongue.

You have reached the age when one is of interest to an adult only insofar as one seems to have a future. The mind of a little child is fascinating, for it looks on old things with new eyes – but at about twelve this changes. The adolescent offers nothing, can do nothing, say nothing that the adult cannot do better. Living with you in Baltimore (and you have told Harold that I alternated between strictness and neglect, by which I suppose you mean the times I was so inconsiderate as to have T.B., or to retire into myself to write, for I had little social life apart from you) represented a rather too domestic duty forced on me by your mother's illness. But I endured your Top Hats and Telephones until the day you snubbed me at dancing school, less willingly after that . . . . To sum up: What you have done to please me or make me proud is practically negligible since the time you made yourself a good diver at camp (and now you are softer than you have ever been). In your career as a "wild society girl," vintage of 1925, I'm not interested. I don't want any of it – it would bore me, like dining with the Ritz Brothers. When I do not feel you are "going somewhere," your company tends to depress me for the silly waste and triviality involved. On the other hand, when occasionally I see signs of life and intention in you, there is no company in the world I prefer. For there is no doubt that you have something in your belly, some real gusto for life – a real dream of your own – and my idea was to wed it to something solid before it was too late – as it was too late for your mother to learn anything when she got around to it. Once when you spoke French as a child it was enchanting with your odd bits of knowledge – now your conversation is a commonplace as if you'd spent the last two years in the Corn Hollow High School – what you saw in *Life* and read in *Sexy Romances*.

I shall come East in September to meet your boat – but this letter is a declaration that I am no longer interested in your promissory notes but only in what I see. I love you always but I am only interested by people who think and work as I do and it isn't likely that I shall change at my age. Whether you will – or want to – remains to be seen.

Daddy

15 months later.

5521 Amestoy Avenue
Encino, California
25 January 1940

Dearest Scottie:

Communication having apparently ceased from your end, I conclude that you are in love. Remember – there's an awful disease that overtakes popular girls at 19 or 20 called emotional bankruptcy. Hope you are not preparing the way for it. Also I have a bill from a doctor which includes an X ray. Have you had a cough? Please give me a little information, no matter how skimpy.

You have earned some money for me this week because I sold "Babylon

Revisited," in which you are a character, to the pictures (the sum received wasn't worthy of the magnificent story – neither of you nor of me – however, I am accepting it).

Dearest love always.

Daddy

1403 North Laurel Avenue

Hollywood, California

2 November 1940

Dearest Scottina:

Listening to the Harvard–Princeton game on the radio with the old songs reminds me of the past that I lived a quarter of a century ago and that you are living now. I picture you as there though I don't know whether you are or not.

I remember once a long time ago I had a daughter who used to write me letters but now I don't know where she is or what she is doing, so I sit here listening to Puccini – "Someday she'll write (Pigliano edda ciano)."

With dearest love,

Daddy

1403 North Laurel Avenue

Hollywood, California

29 November 1940

Dearest Scottina:

I started Tom Wolfe's book on your recommendation. It seems better than *Time and the River*. He has a fine inclusive mind, can write like a streak, has a great deal of emotion, though a lot of it is maudlin and inaccurate, but his awful secret transpires at every crevice – he did not have anything particular to say! That stuff about the GREAT VITAL HEART OF AMERICA is simply just corny.

He recapitulates beautifully a great deal of what Walt Whitman said and Dostoevski said and Nietzsche said and Milton said, but he himself, unlike Joyce and T.S. Eliot and Ernest Hemingway, has nothing really new to add. All right – it's all a mess and it's too bad about the individual – so what? Most writers line themselves up along a solid gold bar like Ernest's courage, or Joseph Conrad's art, or D.H. Lawrence's intense cohabitations, but Wolfe is too "smart" for this and I mean smart in its most belittling and modern sense . . . .

ERNEST HEMINGWAY
1899–1961

Ernest Hemingway was born in a Chicago suburb in 1899. His father Ed, a doctor, took the young Ernest hunting and fishing and instilled in him a love of nature, a sense of competition and pride in his own skills. His mother, Grace represented the artistic side of his nature, teaching music, painting and encouraging her son to play the 'cello. She dominated Ed, whom Ernest came to see as a weak man, a coward, and he rejected this cowardice throughout his life.

Hemingway claimed to have hated his mother for what she did to his father and when Ed shot himself in late 1928 Hemingway wrote to his friend Maxwell Perkins "What makes me feel the worst is that father is the one I cared about."

Hemingway had three sons – John or Bumby by his first wife Hadley, and Patrick (Mouse, Mex) and Gregory (Giggy) by his second, Pauline Pfeiffer, whom he married in 1927. His letters to his young sons show an inability to talk in purely childish tones, preferring instead to talk of his alcoholic bravura and his manly activities in the wilds. Nevertheless, he did pass on his love for nature and pride in skills he himself had mastered.

Ford Madox Ford had advised Hemingway always to write a letter thinking of posterity but Hemingway rejected his own letters as colloquial, full of misspellings and in no way literary. He admitted that he used the letters as a warm-up excercise and for fun – as a means of gathering and spreading gossip.

Here, Hemingway writes to his mother in Kansas City.

16 January 1918

Dear Mother

I just got your letter today. I was beginning to wonder why I didn't hear from the folks but the trains have all been tied up in bad shape. It was 20 degrees below here too tho not so much snow. In Kansas they had two or three feet in most all the country. No trains got thru at all from the West or East. We were cut off for a while. The coal shortage is still pretty bad here. However we should cogitate for it will soon be spring. Now dry those tears Mother and cheer up. You will have to find something better than that to worry about. Don't worry or cry or fret about my not being a good Christian. I am just as much as ever and pray every night and believe just as hard so cheer up! Just because I'm a *cheerful* Christian ought not to bother you.

The reason I don't go to church on Sunday is because I have to work till 1 a.m. getting out the Sunday Star and every once in a while till 3 and 4 a.m. And I never open my eyes Sunday morning until 12.30 noon anyway. So you see it isn't because I don't want to. You know I don't rave about religion but I am a sincere a Christian as I can be. Sunday is the one day in the week that I can get my sleep out. Also Aunt Arabell's church is a very well dressed stylish one with a not to be loved preacher and I feel out of place.

Now Mother I got awfully angry when I read what you wrote about Carl [Edgar] and Bill [Smith]. I wanted to write immediately and say everything I thought. But I waited until I got all cooled off. But never having met Carl and knowing Bill only superficially you *were* mighty unjust. Carl is a *Prince* and about the most sincere and real Christian I have ever known. He doesn't drool at the mouth like a Peaslee with religion but is a deep sincere Christian and gentleman.

I have never asked Bill what church he goes to because that doesn't matter. We both believe in God and Jesus Christ and have hopes for a here-after and creeds don't matter.

Please don't unjustly criticize my best friends again. Now cheer up because I'm not drifting like you thought.

With love,
Ernie

Don't read this to anyone and please get back to a cheerful frame of mind!

TO HIS FATHER

Milan
11 September 1918

Dear Dad:

Your letters of Aug 6th and 11th came today. I'm glad you got that one from Ted and know he will be glad to hear from you. He came in from the front as soon as he knew I was wounded and at the Base here and wrote that letter to you in Milan. It was before my leg had been X–Rayed or operated on and so I don't know just what he told you about it all because I was too sick to give a damn. But I hope it was all right. I had a letter from him from the front a couple of days ago and they are having a good time. Mother wrote that you and she were going up North and I know you had a good vacation. Write me all about it if you did any fishing. That is what makes me hate this war. Last year this time I was making those wonderful catches of Rainbow at the [Horton] Bay.

I'm in bed today and probably won't leave the hospital for about three weeks more. My legs are coming on wonderfully and will both eventually be O.K. absolutely. The left one is all right now. The right is stiff but massage and sun cure and passive movements are loosening up the knee. My surgeon Captain Sammarelli, one of the best surgeons in Italy, is always asking me whether I think that you will be entirely satisfied with the operations. He says that his work must be inspected by the great Surgeon Hemingway of Chicago and he wants it to be perfect. And it is too. There is a scar about 8 inches long in the bottom on my foot and a neat little puncture on top. Thats what copper jacketted bullets do when they "key hole" in you. My knee is a beauty also. I'll never be able to wear kilts Pop. My left leg, thigh and side look like some old horse that has been branded and rebranded by about 50 owners. They will all make good identification marks.

I can get around now on the streets for a little while each day with a cane or crutch, but can't put a shoe on my right foot yet. Oh, yes! I have been commissioned a 1st Lieutenant and now wear the two gold stripes on each of my sleeves. It was a surprise to me as I hadn't expected anything of the sort. So now you can address my mail either 1st Lieut. or Tenente as I hold the rank in both the A.R.C. and Italian Army. I guess I'm the youngest 1st Lieut. in the Army. Anyway I feel all dolled up with my insignia and a shoulder strap on my Sam Brown Belt. I also heard that my silver medaglia valore is on the way and I will probably get as soon as I'm out of the Hospital. Also they brought back word from the Front that I was proposed for the war cross before I was wounded because of general foolish conduct in the trenches, I guess. So maybe I'll be decorated with both medals at once. That would not be bad.

P.S. If it isn't too much I wish you'd subscribe to the Sat. Eve. Post for me and have it sent to my address here. They will forward it to me wherever I am. You need American reading an awful lot when your at the front.

Thanks

Ernie

Hendaye, France
14 September 1927

Dear Dad:

Thanks very much for your letter and for forwarding the letter to Uncle Tyley (Hancock). I had a good letter from him yesterday. You cannot know how badly I feel about having caused you and Mother so much shame and suffering–but I could not write you about all of my and Hadley's troubles even if it were the thing to do. It takes two weeks for a letter to cross the Atlantic and I have tried not to transfer all the hell I have been through to anyone by letter. I love Hadley and I love Bumby–Hadley and I split up – I did not desert her nor was I committing adultery with anyone, I was living in the apartment with Bumby – looking after him while Hadley was away on a trip and it was when she came back from this trip that she decided she wanted the definite divorce. We arranged everything and there was no scandal and no disgrace. Our trouble had been going on for a long time. It was entirely my fault and it is no one's business. I have nothing but love admiration and respect for Hadley and while we are busted up I have not in any way lost Bumby. He lived with me in Switzerland after the divorce and he is coming back in November and will spend this winter with me in the mountains.

You are fortunate enough to have only been in love with one woman in your life. For over a year I had been in love with two people and had been absolutely faithful to Hadley. When Hadley decided that we had better get divorced the girl with whom I was in love was in America. I had not heard from her for almost two months. In her last letter she had said that we must not think of each other but of Hadley. You refer to "Love Pirates," "persons who break up your home etc." and you know that I am hot tempered but I know that it is easy to wish people in Hell when you know nothing of them. I have seen, suffered, and been through enough so that I do not wish anyone in Hell. It is because I do not want you to suffer with ideas of shame and disgrace that I now write all this. We have not seen much of each other for a long time and in the mean–time our lives have been going on and there has been a year of tragedy in mine and I know you can appreciate how difficult and almost impossible it is for me to write about it . . . .

I'm awfully happy you like Bumby. He is my very dear and I hope because of my own mistakes and errors to be ever a better and wiser father to him and to help him avoid things. But I doubt if anyone can teach anyone else much. Anyway he is a fine boy and I hope inside of eight years we can all three go fishing together and you'll see that we are not such tragic figures . . . .

I love you very much and love Mother too and I'm sorry this is such a long letter – it probably doesn't explain anything but you're the only person I've written six pages to since I learned to use a pen and ink. I remember Mother saying once that she would rather see me in my grave than something – I forget what – smoking cigarettes perhaps. If it's of any interest I don't smoke like a furnace. Many times last winter I would have been very content with anything so simple as being in my grave but there were always enough people who would rather not see me in my grave to whom I owed certain responsibilities to make me keep on going. I just mention this so no one will mention seeing me in my grave. Glad to do anything else to oblige. . . .

> To his son, Patrick Hemingway, who was then 5 years old, at sea, on board General Metzinger, Messageries Maritimes. Patrick was nicknamed the Mexican Mouse.

2 December 1933

Dear Old Mex;

Well here we are almost at the southern end of the Red Sea. Tomorrow we will be in the Indian Ocean. The weather is just like Key West on a nice day in winter. Yesterday we saw a big school of big porpoises and many schools of small porpoises.

It was cold and rainy all the way down to Egypt. Then it was hot and fine. Coming through the Suez canal we went right through the desert. We saw lots of Palm trees and Australian pines (like in our yard) whenever there was water. But the rest was mountains and hills and plains of sand. We saw a lot of camels and a soldier riding on a camel made it trot alongside the ship almost as fast as the ship could go. In the canal you have to stop and tie up to the side sometimes to let other ships go by. You would have liked to see the other ship go by and to see the desert. The only birds we saw were some snipe and quite a lot of hawks and a few cormorants and on old blue crane.

I miss you, old Mex, and will be glad to see you again. Will have plenty of good stories to tell you when we come back.

When you get down to Key West remember me to Captain Bra and Mr. Sully (J.B. Sullivan). Give my best to everybody in Piggott.

Go easy on the beer and lay off the hard liquor until I get back.

Don't forget to blow your nose and turn around three times before you go to bed.

Your affectionate papa,

Papa

La Finca Vigia

7 October 1942

Dearest Mousie:

We were awfully glad to get your letter and to hear that you were such a good football player and that school was as good as you had expected. Gigi wrote you about poor Bates dying. It was really awful. He had that same thing that killed Pony, that took so long for him to die, but we gave him all the medicine he should have had and took good care of him and did everything that we could about it. But Gigi felt awful about it and we didn't know how he would stand up under it finally. He took it very well really because he had such good sense and though he loved Bates he knew there was nothing we could do about it. The other thing that helped him out is that Wolfer has got to be such a fine cat and that we have Testor's new baby who is a wonder cat.

He looks just like Boysy except that he is Persian and has long fur and he is as strong as a bear and is built like a wolverine. Testor is lovely with him and takes such good care of him and has purred almost every minute since he has been born. He is three weeks old yesterday and is now able to make a purr–purr and to walk around and is really a marvelous cat . . . .

Mousy, write about school and tell us all about it. We all want to know how it is. Give my love to the H.Fs. and much love to you from all of us.

Much love from

Papa

Will write often. Gigi wrote yesterday. Max Perkins is sending the big book I wrote about [Men at War].

About football – always remember to swing your arms wide when you tackle. Open them wide before you make the tackle and then slam them together hard. Like slapping them together across your chest. Try always to fall sideways so as to protect your balls as in boxing. Wear a jockstrap when you play.

Papa

Divisional Headquarters near Hemmeres, Germany,
15 September 1944

Dearest Mousie,

. . . . Mouse I miss you and the Old Man [Gregory] and Bumby all the time and think a lot about our fine times to come. Have not heard from the old Bum since this last business started but his Colonel promised me to find out about him and I left word at the Ritz he could use my room if he turned up. We have had very hard fighting yest and today but that is to be expected and everything goes as it should. Am writing with the noise of the counter attack going on. I can't write you details but once the campaign is over I will. You will be very proud of what the Division has done and I have never been happier nor had a more useful life ever. Am saving the maps and we will put them up in the trophy room. . . .

In Paris I only had two days semi–free but saw old friends like Sylvia Beach and Picasso and had two fine walks. It cost $100 to take six people to lunch at a moderate restaurant so we usually cooked on a gas stove in room at the Ritz.

When I was in such bloody awful shape in London – have to sleep flat on back with tins on each side because head would go if it turned sideways. Capa's girl Pinkie was awfully good to me and so was another fine girl named Mary Welsh. I saw her again in Paris and we had a fine time. Think you would like. Have nicknamed Papa's Pocket Rubens. If gets any thinner will promote to pocket Tintoretto. You will have to go to Metropolitan Museum to get the references. Very fine girl. Looked after me in worst time I ever had.

Mouse, my boy, if we last through next two weeks we will have a wonderful life.

Right now I have lost my Burberry rain–coat (it rains all yest) have a battle jacket with the zipper broken held together by safety pins, wear same two shirts worn last two months, both at once, have head cold, chest cold, trouble on both flanks, shelling the Bejesus behind, shelling the ditto ahead, counter attack on our right, what–all on our left and never felt happier. Except wish had some nosedrops for head cold. Am drinking some kind of strange German Schnapps and it looks like will be fine day tomorrow.

Will you pass on to Giggy any of this he is grown up enough to take – and work hard be good guy (you are) and love Papa and know he loves you and will see you in N.Y. before Christmas and will all be together. If headmaster asks tell him Papa actually *Did* go abroad and to various countries there. Best love Moose.

Papa

Hürtgen Forest
19 November 1944

Dearest Mouse:

. . . .Moose don't know what else to write. Paris beautiful but still bad chow situation. Bicycle racing going on. Very fine new riders. Harry's Bar open – but only at 5 pm and no whiskey nor any but phony gin. Papa still living at the Ritz (joint we took) when back in town. Town so lovely but with the exchange 50 to 1 dollar (when really worth about 200 francs to 1 dollar) that very terribly expensive. None of the great pictures on exhibition. Lots of fine new very fine pictures by Picasso and other good painters. Under Krauts painters had nothing to do but stay home and paint. Worked out quite well. Made fine pictures. No oysters yet at Prunier's. It will need a year or so at least to straighten out properly.

Mouse excuse worthless letter. Today very busy day trip up in the woods – awfully sorry to miss Thanksgiving – But lately we've been missing pretty much everything. But we will get it all back with interest. You have the passports fixed – write me vacation dates day you get this.

Much love
Papa

MOTHERS AND
DAUGHTERS ABROAD

1914-1977

KAREN BLIXEN
1885-1962

Karen Blixen, whose maiden name was Isak Dinesen, was Danish and born in 1885. After studying art at Copenhagen, Paris and Rome, she married her cousin, Baron Bror Blixen–Finecke, in 1914. Together they went to Kenya to manage a coffee–plantation. After their divorce in 1921 she continued to run the plantation, advised by her uncle back home in Denmark. A collapse in the coffee market forced her back to Denmark in 1931. Her letters written home during this period have been published under the title *Letters from Africa* and her account of her experiences in Kenya is recorded in her book *Out of Africa*, published in 1937.

Karen Blixen was very close to her mother, Ingeborg Dinesen, and found time to write her a stream of letters. She was, however, very frustrated by the constant family criticism reported to her by her mother. She came from a large, close–knit family and despite the distance between Kenya and Denmark it was apparent from her letters that she felt, at times, they were breathing down her neck, dogging her every move. Obviously Karen's letters were passed around the family and Karen got exasperated that she could not tell her mother anything in confidence. This letter written sometime in 1914 is an example.

. . . . I promise to write to you straight away . . . . but you must promise me not to mention it because I always think it rather embarrassing when there is talk of an expected child so far in advance. But another thing is that I think it would be best if it did not come about for the time being. You may think it would be lovely to have a grandchild; but really Africa is most unsuitable for small children, at least until one has grown a little accustomed to conditions here and is acclimatized. The two other white women on the farm, Mrs

Gethin and Fru Holmberg, are expecting babies now and are in despair, ill and hysterical and always wailing about the *awful nuisance* it is to have a child. I think that is a pity, and that it is better to wait. I certainly would not be suitable on this safari life and that is really Africa's greatest charm. But I promise you to write at once when it happens . . . .

> In another letter she shows how she needs her mother as a confidant. She was going through increasingly difficult times with her husband, Bror and the hoped for baby hadn't arrived.

Ngong
26.7.21

 . . . . Dearest Mother, I find it so hard to write about my private affairs, but I must just send you a couple of lines. During these six months I have come to realize that I am very, very reluctant to separate from Bror. There is so much here that binds us together, and it is impossible for me to stop believing in the good in him, and to think that his various inexplicably thoughtless and heartless outbursts are other than a kind of frenzy, that should surely subside. Perhaps it is simply that I care too much for him; I feel that I cannot abandon him now, when things are so difficult for him . . . .

Karen Estates
P.O. Box 223, Nairobi
Kenya Colony
Ngong
(Autumn 1921)

My own beloved beloved wonderful little Mother.

I have not been able to write to you for so long, and I know very well that that is not right. But everything has been so uncertain, and there have been so many trying things. But that is going to be changed now.

Now I want to beg you earnestly that in future– perhaps for a year, but perhaps not for so long, – I may feel that I am able to write to *you only*, without any one else reading my letters. I am quite aware that the others take such a part in how my affairs are going, and in my joys and sorrows, that they will be hurt by this; but it must be like this for a time; for otherwise I have come to realize that as God is my witness it is utterly impossible for me to write. It is not that I am not just as much attached to them, but in these times, with a fearful drought here, worse than in 1918, and with all my shauries with Bror and so on and so on and so on, – I just cannot have the feeling that my marriage and my money affairs and my future and my state of mind and my bills are being discussed at Matrup and Leerbaek and Holbaek Ladegaard, – or anyway not every single word that I might write to you in a momentary loss of self–control.

Also it is impossible for me to reply to their letters in the way they would like. I am having a terrible time out here; I am involved in so many things, – both purely practical and also where my feelings, my life itself are concerned, – possibly by my own fault or perhaps quite by chance, that it is going to take all my strength if I am to get through them or over them; you are all well aware of this. I believe that I am going to get through; there may well come a time when I feel that I am the happiest of us all and that it will have been worth all the trouble. But as the situation is now, and as every day I have need of all the strength I can muster in order to manage things, I cannot enter into discussion about it with a whole crowd of young and older women and uncles and brothers-in-law and friends.

If I know that I can write to you alone, I will tell you everything I am thinking about; all my plans, when I have any, will be for you to hear, but I must be absolutely sure that you will not show my letters to anyone, without one single exception . . . .

. . . . I see now that I ought not to have gone home last time; it was unnatural and in fact separated me more from you all rather than bringing me closer. It may well be that I will not go home again for a considerable time. I have been wondering, if I can get away from here for a while, whether you and I could not spend a few months in France, for instance, in Paris and the south? For after all it is you who represent "home" to me and all that I love best in Denmark.

I think my greatest misfortune was Father's death. Father understood me as I was, although I was so young, and loved me for myself. It would have been better, too, if I had spent more time with his family I felt more free and at ease with them. I feel that Mama and Aunt Bess and the whole of your family, – and Uncle Aage when he was out here, – if they care for me at all, do so in a way in spite of of my being as I am. They are always trying to change me into something quite different; they do not like the parts of me that I believe to be good . . . .

No doubt each one of your children thinks that he or she loves you most, and so do I. It is probably not true. But each one cares for you in his or her own way, and I think that there is something in the way that I love you that resembles the way Father loved you. For me you are the most beautiful and wonderful person in the world; merely the fact that you are alive makes the whole world different; where you are there is peace and harmony, shade and flowing springs, birds singing; to come to where you are is like entering "heaven." . . . .

These *are* difficult times for me, far, far more difficult than, for instance, when I was ill here. Your love and understanding are lights and stars shining and sparkling through them. And I have to take them in my own way; otherwise I will die of them, you must understand that. And I am sure you have the strength, little Mother, to keep this understanding in spite of others' condemnation. Uncle Aage's grass–house and office work, and Aunt Bess's comparisons between me and the Major's wife, etc. – for heaven's sake, in these times that is sheer rubbish, for this is deadly earnest.

When they talk like this, then listen to them and say yes and amen, but smile in your heart of hearts. Don't let them make you see it in their way; understand me, as only *you* can. And imagine Father is sitting beside you perhaps talking anxiously too about this child of yours out here and saying that she has used up too much money and been improvident in many ways, but perhaps he might see some sense in it as well and would say: "But she is brave, and she loves you and me more, perhaps, than any of our other children; give her a little more time, then you'll see that she will manage." – Yes, talk about me to Father. It is really he who is responsible, for he deserted me and must have seen that things were not going to be easy for me.

But do not discuss me with the others; just let them say what they like, and let me write to you alone. For I love you so very deeply.

A thousand, thousand thanks for paying Borre. That was far too good and kind. But you really must not pay anything else. Of course it is frightful that I have so many debts. But it will all work out.

. . . . Now I must end for today. Next time I will write about my "plans," both present and future.

Goodbye, my dearest dear Mother. I feel you taking me into your arms now. And so I will write to you alone.

Your Tanne.

Ngong
25/10.192(1)

My own beloved Mother.

This time I am writing, as I said to you in my last letter, with the thought that only you will read this. It is so necessary for me to know this that I don't think that I could write at all if I did not feel assured of it. You must not make any exception of any of my letters, even if they should not contain anything secret of confidential. I need so much to have the feeling *always* that I can write about everything to you.

I am going to beg you, dearest Mother, not to write to me any more concerning my marriage or Bror. Of course I know you do it with the best intentions; but sometimes even things done in this spirit can fail, and what costs you effort and pain to write, costs me effort and pain to read, and I do not think anything is gained by it other that my realization of how little you understand me. Or I believe that in this matter,– which in no way should ever have been the subject of general family discussion,– you have talked yourselves into such a state that you have lost sight of any impartial or objective view of it and are judging it completely out of context. My little Mother, you must not think that I am writing in anger or bitterness; but I think that this is the reason for even you writing as you do and I do so deeply wish that it would stop.

. . . . There are two things that none of you understand: how different from you I am and always have been. What makes me happy or unhappy is completely different from what makes you happy or unhappy. I could live in conditions that you would think frightful and be happy, and in conditions which you would think perfect I would be miserable. And you cannot make judgments in advance regarding these conditions; you do not know and can never know what effect they will have on my state of satisfaction, and thus you ought to be careful about the advice you give; you might come to regret it most deeply. For instance, to me my illness was not such an enormous disaster, indeed, if I had not still been under your influence I would have thought it even less of one; but I was constantly aware of the sorrow it would cause you. I actually enjoyed being in the hospital, although it was a hellish cure. No doubt it would have been quite a different matter for one of the others. But not for anything in the world would I go back to the time when I had to go to Folehave for dinner every Sunday. You must not think this is written out of hard–heartedness. I would really rather leave it alone; but it *cannot* be avoided when you write as you do, and I think that you have written things to me now that have hurt me still more, and this is the only way that I can think of the put a stop to it from both sides.

. . . . Now it is my fervent hope and constant thought that all of you at home will approve my plan for dividing up the farm and reorganizing the management. I have been thinking about it day and night during the last few months, and I believe it is good. I really do think, – don't say that I have *folie de grandeur*, – that if you will allow me to be in charge of this farm and give me a free hand there will not be another farm in B.E.A. to match up with it. It is because I take such a passionate interest in it. Hunter laughs at me, – but I love it, every acre, every native, every coffee bush . . . .

Dearest Mother, please understand this letter, which is written in the greatest, greatest, greatest most fervently deep love . . . . then you will truly understand how I tremble at the possibility of these misunderstandings becoming real. Understand, that I do *not* want that to happen, not for anything in the world or the next; I would rather never see any of you again than that. And as Doune said: Remember when you ride you are holding *on to a mouth*, – I say to you, remember, when you write, that you are striking a heart. And then remember how far away from you all that I am; the effect is so different at such a distance. As Cyrano says:"Je mourai si de cette hauteur Vous me laissez tomber un mot dur sur le coeur." . . . .

Goodnight, my above all else beloved Mother.

Your Tanne.

The difficulty Karen and her mother have in understanding each other and the lengthy correspondence they have discussing this matter goes on for some time. The large Dinesen family get in the way of trust and communication between mother and daughter. They all appear to have very definite opinions on Karen's problems and are not backwards in expressing them to Ingeborg who then reports to her daughter. The feeling that they were all against her must have been very alienating, being so far away and unable to speak up for herself. The last straw came when she learnt that the entire family had assembled (in Denmark) to discuss whether she and Bror should get divorced. In anger and humiliation she wrote home to her mother suggesting that it would be better if for the time being they didn't correspond and that if she received a letter from her mother she said that she wouldn't open it.

. . . . But of course you will hear my business letters to Uncle Aage each month. I have given thought to the idea of leaving this farm; and perhaps it is a weakness in me not to do so. But I am staying because I am convinced that if I left it would fail. And it is not merely the thought of your money that makes me wish to prevent this happening because of some step on my part, but because it is my life's work and I cannot relinquish it. The natives here, who rely on me, everything, even our oxen and our coffee trees – I could never think about them with the knowledge that I had deserted them. If you do not wish me to stay, whether you say so directly, or, by some demand or other that my pride and my self–esteem will not allow me to comply with, drive me away, then it will be your responsibility. I know now that I cannot take it, and I am writing this to you in explanation of what may seem incomprehensible to you all, my staying on here.

And now goodbye, my dearest, dearest, dearest Mother. I cannot tell you how deeply I love you, how much I will always bless you.

Your Tanne.

In fact, Karen Blixen never really stopped writing to her mother and the very next month she sent a loving, emotional letter saying how often she thought of all their friends and relatives in Denmark and how she was missing them. On 23rd January 1922 she added an addendum to a letter to her mother:

Beloved Mother.

I am adding a couple of lines to my letter to tell you that I am probably going to take the step you so much wish for; Bror and I are going to be divorced. I would ask you not to talk about it, but I wanted to tell you. Please understand that the decision has not been made before because Bror has been in such a terrible situation here. He has been without work and money, wanted by the police; he has been hiding out in the Masai Reserve without a tent or shoes. It was impossible for me, in consideration of other people here and of myself, to start to talk of divorce. But I think that things we'll go better with him now; he is probably going to get married, as soon as it can be arranged, to an English lady who wants to help him.

I am bound to say that it is very hard to look back at a whole period of one's life and have to admit: it came to nothing. But apart from this, and the actual pain of parting from someone I have loved so much, I think I will come to feel it as a relief from many impossible situations. . . .

NELLIE GRANT
1881–1977

Nellie Grant wrote regularly to her daughter Elspeth Huxley from 1944 to 1977 whilst she was living in Africa and her daughter was in England.

She was born in Berkhamsted in Hertfordshire, the sixth and youngest daughter of Lord Richard de Aquila Grosvenor. Nellie was a clever girl and could have shone academically, but on leaving school she was required to go home and be daughter of the house. When she was 21 she married a Scotsman, Josceline Grant, eleven years her senior and a bit of a wanderer. Their only daughter, Elspeth, was born in London, but soon afterwards, in 1912, Jos and Nellie made the decision to emigrate to what was then British East Africa. They had little money and the only preparation that Nellie made for the life of a pioneer was to take a course in poultry keeping.

Once in Africa, they bought five hundred acres of land at Thika for £4 an acre. Thika was about thirty miles north of Nairobi and was rough grass, scrub and bush. By mid 1914 sixty acres of coffee had been planted and land prepared for more, but by the end of the year Jos returned to England to rejoin The Royal Scots and after a few months of running the farm on her own, Nellie had to return too. In 1919 they were to return to Thika and Nellie was to remain there until 1965, two years after this corner of the Empire had become the independent Republic of Kenya.

Elspeth returned to England to go to Reading University and after she had completed her degree she did not return to Africa but married Gervas Huxley. They both visited Kenya in 1933 but returned in June of that year, after which Nellie wrote weekly letters from 1933 until her death in 1977, reflecting, as she said, "the minutiae of life, the small beer, not the 'Big Bow Wow'". . . .

30 October 1934

. . . . Graded rabbit wool all morning, and an unknown girl arrived about 4pm. She is a daughter of a pseudo-friend of my youth who married a half-wit of the great Cecil clan. She got engaged to someone considered unsuitable, so was sent out here for a year. At first I thought she was an awful girl, very pleased with herself, long-winded and platitudinous, but when she got on to describing the awfulness and fatuosity of her mother, I liked her better – Gall-sickness is terribly bad now, I lost two cows and two calves last week.

Absolutely no rain which is damnable, how long the pyrethrum can go on as it is I tremble to think. I have over thirty thousand plants in a trench waiting to go out, and haven't had anything approaching a single planting day since August.

> Nellie had been asking Elspeth for photographs of her grandson; some now arrived.

24 July 1944

. . . . I think the snaps are entrancing. I shall now enter Speke's grocery with head erect and flashing eye, facing my cronies with confidence. Have been so much put to shame by always hearing "What? No snaps yet?"

> In April 1947 Jos, Nellie's husband died in Nakuru Hospital. Nellie returned to the farm and resumed her letters.

28 July 1947

I appeal to you in the name of humanity, plus that of a mother, to do something about the music as laid on by the BBC via N'bi. Sat. evening at 8.30pm surely ought to have something cheerful? The Announcer said it would be Dido who, having ordered the building of her funeral pyre, was bidding farewell to her devoted attendant. Dido then shrieked: "Farewell Belinda, farewell Belinda", about two dozen times. I wish we could have heard Belinda's reactions, which I feel would have been:"Thank Gawd the old girl has gone and set 'erself alight." When Dido had incinerated herself beyond power of being able to shriek any longer to Belinda, we had a Fugue from King Arthur, which was gloom personified and completely lacking in charm. I gave up then; tried again yesterday when a sonata of Chopin's sounded promising; it turned out to be a Funeral March played by Sergius Rachmaninoff.

The next letter is written after reading the typescript of her daughter's book, *The Flame Trees of Thika*, based on Elspeth's childhood experiences in Kenya.

8 July 1958

Have read two–thirds of the typescript and like it very much. I am *not* like Tilly. Very nostalgic, all the African part – The most noticeable tree at Thika was the *Erythrina tomentosa*, the sealing-wax tree, with corky looking trunk and brilliant red flowers which happen when the leaves are off. They were wild all over the place. I had very good roses in the garden which came from a grower at Orleans in a huge crate – only three pence each! . . . .

I think you were ever so nice to the Africans in the book. I only remember one episode when any real gratitude was shown. An old man was brought in obviously with bad pneumonia, for which of course there was nothing in those days like M & B. So I made him comfortable in the bathroom of the old grass hut. We went to dine at Kichanga's and got back about 1 am when the old man appeared to be quite dying, so I gave him half a bottle of neat brandy. Next morning he was round the corner, and he brought me eggs as gifts for years . . . .

Could you get for Betty to bring out a *very* thick pair of men's long woolly pants to the ankle? I want them as an Xmas present to old Manvi who gets perished with cold coping with the irrigation at night.

7 May 1961

I am sure you will have read in the home press about this ghastly murder at the Osbornes on Friday night. It looks horribly like a really true-to-type Mau Mau murder, as it wasn't for food or money. The only *non*-Mau Mau aspect is that they didn't rush upstairs and kill the two babies. I think the brave chap was the house-boy who ran two miles to fetch neighbours when he heard David's cries for help.

Later. Just been summoned to a special meeting of the Njoro Settlers Assn. re the Osborne tragedy. I can't see what they can do, but shall go as I rather think I've got the wrong ammunition in my gun. As I couldn't find my ammunition I told the police I'd accidentally put it down the old *choo*, so got a permit for more. Now I've found the old stuff and it looks quite different from the new.

13 February 1965

I disagree entirely with your attitude to Winston's funeral, in fact sternly disapprove of the suggestion that 'the old man's wake' was overplayed. For a few hours millions of people were gouged out of their filthy little runnels of cynicism, sneering and money-grubbing, and actually worshipped and did homage to greatness. It all gave England a spiritual boost, goodness knows how much needed, so I am sorry you wrote as you did.

At the age of 92 this remarkable woman returned to England for treatment and Nellie seized the opportunity to pursue her new interest in puppetry, talking to experts and buying all the materials she would need for making them back in the Algarve, where she was then living.

9 July 1977

Leg is getting on fine, but arthritic knee's the devil. I do *badly* need four packets of plasticine, any colour, to continue puppet masks. Each mask takes two or three days to dry out – I hope you can read this, I can't. Now, on another subject. If I depart this life, don't worry. No case of suicide, haven't the guts, but five chums went out pouf, like that, so why, in the words of the old song, oh why, shouldn't it be poor little me. I would really sooner get it all over and done with, a horrid time for you clearing up I know but that has to be anyway, so *don't* grieve unduly, see? Church fete this morning. Am not there. Poor Phyl the queen-pin.

Nellie seems to be the ideal mother, interested in her children and grandchildren but not interfering; pursuing her own interests and, until the very end, staunchly independent.

FREYA STARK
1893–1993

Freya Stark was an intrepid traveller who wrote numerous books on her experiences in Iran, Iraq, southern Arabia and Asia Minor. She was also an indefatigable writer of letters and published four volumes of autobiography. She was born in Paris and spent her early childhood with her parents on Dartmoor. However, when she was eight years old, her half-Genoese mother took a house at Asolo, some 40 miles north-west of Venice and this was to remain her home, in the intervals between her travels, for the rest of her life. Freya Stark travelled for a number of reasons. She was unashamedly romantic and loved the ancient civilisations and was also fascinated by people and new situations. This is vividly illustrated in her travel writing and in her letters.

Like Karen Blixen, she was very close to her mother and wrote regularly to her, confiding her inmost thoughts and experiences. As a young woman she became engaged to Professor Quirino (Guido) Ruata to whom she refers in the following letters, but the engagement was broken. In 1947 she married Stewart Peronne, an orientalist historian and colonial administrator. The marriage was only short-lived.

Despite her adventurous and often dangerous journeys in an age when women were not expected to travel alone, Freya retained an endearing love of clothes and her femininity. "Nothing," she wrote in her autobiography, "is more useful to a woman traveller than a genuine interest in clothes: it is a key to unlock the hearts of women of all ages and races..." Her letters are full of descriptions of what she wore and requests to her mother to send her some item of fashion.

The following group of letters are written during the First World War.

1 February 1914

My dear my own Mother,

I feel I have had so much more than I deserve, and now I am quite bewildered and overpowered. It is so good to feel that one is loved – the only real riches in the world, and I am very happy in that. I think my soul came to me quite suddenly, when I was about eleven years old, and all at once I realised how precious you were to me – since then have we not been growing nearer and nearer? When we go to the next world I hope St. Peter will not know which is which.

Here are some of my birthday flowers as a remembrance.

Freya

Dronero (Piedmont)
30 March 1915

My dearest Mother,

I arrived here quite exhausted, about 12.30 – after an hour's delay between Parma and Reggio because a *vagone* had got heated and had to be taken off. There was certainly no fear of solitude for me: we had eight people per compartment and a file down the corridors almost all the way, and most objectionable people too.

I got a pretty black hat – straw under and a silk covering, with a tiny rose-bunch. It has a brim and is worn rakishly on one side. Twenty-two francs: and very ladylike and distinguished.

The Bisolfis were charming to me: he was such as dear and so affectionate and good, and he wants to be our *testimonio* too! The first thing he did when I entered the studio was to embrace me and ask: 'Ebbene, quando ti sposi' He says he will be a lot in Bologna about the monument, and that he wants to see a lot of us.

Your Freya

FREYA STARK TO HER MOTHER

11 Grove End Rd.
28 October 1916

My own darling B,

It is fine news to think of having a mackintosh! It's the only thing needed. Now I wonder if you can send me my best hat, the black: I am badly in need of it. The little green one makes me look so *very* old: and my funds are too low to buy one for some time to come. Also the old black velvet and fur if still decent? If I earn any money this winter I want to give it it Viva, as everyone is very poor and I had rather not be a burden.

I go on Wednesday to be interviewed at the War Office and hope to turn out favourably, although German is the only language that is really wanted.

On Wednesday we went to Mrs. Scott's for a soldiers' tea: convalescents, almost all with their heads bandaged as is usually the case this year. I wish the poor boys in Italy could be treated a little as they are here: they do have a good time! They were allowed tea by themselves (forty-six of them), and then we joined them, and they were given cigarettes, and entertainments; I don't think they cared much to be sung to, but loved to get up and do it themselves, and to join in the choruses. I don't know why it makes one want to cry always. Tipperary is no longer: we now sing 'If I were the only girl in the world, and you were the only boy!' – or 'Pack up your troubles in your old kit bag, and smile, smile, smile,' of which the moral was good, though much out of tune.

I rarely see the dear Professor, he is so busy, but he ran in for a moment some days ago, and gave me a beautiful book of Tuscan folk songs – little gems!

Did I announce to you my intention of joining Trevelyan's unit in the spring? I hope you approve, and notice my virtue in postponing till then. Probably I shan't be able to get out there anyway, it is so much sought after.

Your own
Freya

11 Grove End Rd.
12 July 1917

My own darling,

I am just out of bed after inoculation, and am now off to the dentist; and all this for the service of one's country. Who would not rather go to the front straightaway?

We had a thrilling time on Saturday with the big raid. Viva first noticed the exceptionally loud banging of the guns; we went out by the front door, and there were about twenty Taubes coming straight for us from Highgate way, clearly defined in black against a grey cloudy sky. By the time they were nearly over us, our own aircraft were up, their formation was broken, and a number of separate duels were going on, with a great noise all round as if the ground were bubbling up in a series of spasms. The shrapnel was falling all round Selfridges, so that they were quite near; and looked more so being monster machines of a special type. Altogether we counted any number between thirty and fifty by the end, and they drove away like a flock of starlings. We retreated to the kitchen when they appeared to be right over-head, but then went up to the drawing room to see; and got a splendid view.

A loving kiss from
Freya

After the war Freya resumed her travelling and in the thirties spent much time in the Middle East. She continued her correspondence with her mother, confiding in her, describing the life in Arabia and again expressing the delight she took in pretty clothes. Her vivid accounts of domestic detail paints a scene which brings to life the Arab world and her struggles as a courageous female traveller coping with the prejudices of what is acceptable for a woman.

Baghdad
6 December 1929

Dearest B,

Feeling *very* homesick. I sent you a telegram the other day for my fancy dress, for Mrs. Drower tells me I shall be going to a dance at New Year, but I do not know: at present I am feeling uncomfortable, as all the people I meet (except dear Mrs. Drower and Mrs Caparn) are rather suspicious of me and have been asking whether I am a spy. I fear it will be very hard to keep in favour with both Arab and British, and the tragedy is that we seem to have brought a whiff of our own snobbishness among the Iraqis: I find that those I come upon independently are much nicer and more genuine than those I know through British introductions.

. . . . Today was a blustering rainy day and my teacher, packed very tight in a raincoat which swathed him without a crease (except a few horizontal ones), came for me at two, and we launched out into the choppy muddy expanse of the Tigris with great difficulty, the stairs being coated down the bank with very slippery mud which began to suck you in slowly as you stood on the jumping off place. I got on board before it closed over my ankles, and we had a fine spin down the river and no real wetting though the teacher assured his family that "we took refuge with God from the strength of the water". Last week he told me that in summer all Iraqis who wear European clothers "take refuge with God from the discomfort of their socks" – a piteous thought . . . .

Your
Freya

Hamadan
6 May 1930

Darling B,

Don't know why but I am so very depressed this evening – feeling so old, and as if my whole life were wasted and now it were too late to do anything with it: such an uphill work, with so much less health and strength and power than most and already half way through and nothing done. And as if what I *do* do were not worth doing: no one seems to think it is, but just wonder at me and are sorry for me if they are nice, and disapprove if they are not. To be just middle-aged with no particular charm or beauty and no position is a dreary business. In fact I feel as if I had been going uphill all the time to nowhere in particular, and – like poor Venetia – most dreadfully lonely, envying all these women with their nice clean husbands whose tradition is their tradition, and their nice flaxen children who will carry it on in the same simple and steady way. And though it *is* my tradition too, no one thinks it is, because of a silly difference of form and speech and fashion – so that I feel as if I *had* no people of my own. If only I could eventually find some work that would make me feel settled and interested. I hope it may be: but no one seems to want women very much – and I don't quite know that I am fit for anything but philanthropy, and that would not really thrill me. Well, I think it must be because no one any longer makes love to me except when they are drunk.

I went yesterday to call on the Governor's wife and two daughters. It was quite pleasant: their manners very agreeable, and our Persian just enough to be able to talk about pilgrimages, curios, and silver work: they had some really lovely specimens of the Isfahan work which is so hideous when not very good. We sat round the walls and sipped little glasses of tea and had about half a dozen silver dishes of biscuits, cake, sweets, preserved cherries, all placed within reach. It is rude to go away before one has had two glasses of tea. Then you say 'Will you command our excuse. We have given so much trouble,' and go.

. . . . I feel that I really may end by doing something; only it is not a thing that can be hurried. But in three years time I could know enough Persian, Turkish, Kurdish, and Arabic to get about, and I believe I would be the only English woman in the Near East to do so: and then something amusing is bound to turn up. As it is, another six months here will give me Persian: it is most comforting to find how easy these languages are after Arabic. It is merely a matter of learning the words. If only I had a better memory it would be such a blessing.

Dearest love to you both.

Your

Freya

Baghdad

25 October 1932

Darling B,

The dresses have come! I felt like Cinderella opening the box, and don't yet know myself. They are too lovely and I have already twice worn the black and white day frock – just now to the Queen's garden party. The shoes fit *perfectly*, and all the beads are *lovely*. Thanks *so* much dear B. It is gorgeous, receiving all those clothes and so chic; it felt so nice to be really well dressed this afternoon.

The garden party was in honour of four female delegates from the 'Woman's International League': one talkative old English woman, a tall Frenchwoman like a Grenadier just spoilt in the making: a little Syrian, very small and shrinking like a drowned rat, only obstinate: and the President, a fat plain lady Druse from Lebanon with little corkscrew curls under a black veil, always worrying about being first. They are having meetings and making a great flutter about women's rights and progress, and the Arab men, I hear, all dislike it very much. The garden party was a great success however, and was on the lawns of the King's palace, all pleasantly set out with little tables, and when the two Queens arrived the band – which the King had lent as a great concession – struck up the national anthem – for the first time for a woman – and the Queens with a select circle sat at the chief table where they had a chocolate cake with a crown on it.

Your own
Freya

EXILE AND THE SECOND WORLD WAR

1931–1944

SIR HANS KREBS F.R.S.
1900–1981

Hans Krebs, the Jewish scientist, left Germany in order to study at Cambridge University in June 1933. His father was very sad that circumstances had forced his son to leave Germany. He loved Germany and was deeply attached to German civilization – its literature, music, fine arts, sciences and scholarship. He admired the idealized virtues personified by Frederick the Great and Bismarck: self-discipline, a sense of duty, reliability, integrity, candour, diligence, tolerance, fairness, and moral and physical courage. He expressed his feeling in a letter to Hans a few days before his departure.

My dear Hans,

Before you leave German soil, I want to send you warmest greetings and wishes. Would that you will find abroad still more recognition and good fortune that has been accorded you in your homeland. I hope that we shall see each other not less frequently than hitherto – be it in England, be it in Germany. I have even started to learn some English (from Maria) although my 66-year-old tongue does not find it easy to cope with the unfamiliar and peculiar pronunciation. Very earnestly I beseech you to write more frequently than you have in the past, and also in more detail. Especially let me know soon exactly what the position is that you are going to. Is it a teaching post or a research appointment? What will the salary be and what are your prospects?

There is nothing new to report from us, nor from Lise and Wolf in Berlin. There was a comment in the Frankfurter Zeitung which seemed to indicate that the elimination of Jews from the AEG* has not finished yet.

*General Electric Company where his brother Wolfgang was employed

One final point: If you do well abroad, which is my sincere wish and hope, do not forget your brother and sister in Germany, and above all little Gisela and her mother. It may be that you will be called upon to be their shield and succour.

I embrace you most affectionately

Sadly, Hans Kreb's father did not visit him in England, but died of a heart attack in Germany in 1939. It was, perhaps, a blessing that he was spared the shame of what was to take place in the following years of the Second World War. However, Hans' step-mother and step-sister joined him in England but were subsequently caught in Germany in 1939 on holiday and were forced to remain there. They both survived the war. His brother came to England before the war and his sister and brother-in-law emigrated to Israel.

Krebs – the name is familiar to generations of medical and biochemistry students as the discoverer of the 'Krebs citric acid cycle'– remained in England to pursue a long and distinguished career in Cambridge, Sheffield and Oxford. He was elected to the Royal Society in 1942 and awarded the Nobel Prize for Medicine in 1958. He remained active in research, as Emeritus Professor of Biochemistry in Oxford, until his death aged 81.

HERBERT LEVY
b.1929

The separation of Jewish families was a tragic feature of the war. The story of Herbert Levy is typical.

Herbert Levy was born in Berlin in July 1929. When he was nearly 10 years old, he was sent by *Kindertransport* (June 1939) to England in order to escape the persecution by the Nazis. Herbert remembers the build up to the war, in particular *Kristallnacht*. The day after this, the Nazis came to arrest his Grandfather who lived with his Grandmother in the apartment next door. His Grandfather was 85 years old and very ill so the police turned their attention to Herbert's father, questioning him but then departing. Herbert's father decided it would be safer to live with one of Herbert's uncles who had an English passport and lived in Berlin. Herbert and his mother moved out of their own apartment and joined the grandparents.

Kindertransport was a response to the program, *Kristallnacht*. It was part of the Movement for the Care of Children from Germany and was an attempt to rescue Jewish children by transporting them to England before the war broke out. It was organised by Jews in England and

162

Germany with the agreement of the German government. Children had to be under 16 years of age in order to qualify for a place. Herbert Levy was one of those children.

They were allowed to take with them a very limited amount of luggage and one mark in money. This had to be spent before arriving at the border. Herbert Levy still remembers this today, because, he says, he had about 15 Pfennigs left and "as we neared the border I was afraid I would be found with these few coins, so I threw them out of the train window."

The reception centre in England was at Harwich where volunteers picked out children and took them home. The children often felt lonely and alienated, far away from all that they knew and understood. Some children, including Herbert, were then taken to a gymnasium near Liverpool Street in London. Although many children would be placed in non-Jewish families, Herbert's case was a little different as he had an uncle living in North London and thus a home to go to. However, he was only 10 years old, spoke no English and was separated from his parents.

Fortunately they were able to follow him in August 1939, though they were delayed by the death of Herbert's grandfather on 18th July 1939. They were only allowed to bring out 10 Reichsmark – about £25 at today's prices but they completed the immigration procedures and all squeezed together in his uncle's house. However, more upheavals were to come. Later that year he was evacuated to Yaxley, near Peterborough, where he was taken in by the local vicar and then later he and his mother were placed in an internment camp on the Isle of Man.

Throughout all these separations Herbert Levy wrote letters and cards. He even wrote a play about the situation on his arrival in England. Sadly, his grandmother, with whom he and his mother had lived in Berlin, died at Auschwitz.

The letters were of course written in German and have been translated by Herbert Levy. Through the letters of this little boy we pick up threads of the tragedy being acted out; a tragedy of far-reaching consequences, involving countless Jewish families living in Europe. This is the story of one particular family caught by circumstances in the mayhem of the Second World War.

Herbert Levy matriculated in England and did his National Service where he was in the Education Corps. He did a lot of acting and at one point was offered a part in a film, starring Jean Simmons, but he was refused a work permit. He broadcast with the World Service, wrote two plays for children and had walk-on parts with Sadlers Wells Opera Company. Later he went into business to support his wife, Lily, who had herself been in Bergen-Belsen, and his two children, but he maintained his love of the theatre and has never stopped writing.

The following letter was written by Herbert Levy to his parents on landing at Harwich in June 1939.

Dear Parents,

I have about an hour here. Sorry I did not write to you from Hook – that card went to Karlsruhe. I and 9 other children are sitting in the Customs place in Harwich. I am very happy and I am well. I was not sea-sick on the ship.
Lots of love and kisses – Herbert.

For a boy of 10 years old, in a strange country, Herbert settled down stoically and optimistically to await the arrival of his parents. He soon settled in, helping his uncle in the garden and enjoying trips to places of interest.

26 June 1939

Dear family,

We have today received the letter with the key to the suitcase; we do not yet know how we are going to collect the things from the station.

Yesterday, Sunday, we went with Mr Carr's motor to Windsor Castle from where I sent you a postcard. It is very nice here although the weather is not too good; it will start to rain at any moment. There is a lovely garden here where I can play the whole day, water the flowers, the gardener also looks after Uncle Joszi's stock – each day I collect the shillings and the pennies. I have also seen the room that you, dear parents, will have once you arrive here. It is very sunny and has a built-in cupboard. The room that we have at present will be for the grandparents. It is very suitable for Grandad because it is on the ground floor. Next year we shall clear an area in the garden, then Grandad can always sit in the fresh air.

I could still write a lot, but the others want to add their bit.
Love and kisses – Herbert

The next month he sends birthday good wishes to his mother and in a separate note, some advice on what to bring when they come to England.

Dear Mummy,

I send my congratulations to you today because I do not want to write to you tomorrow. So, dear Mummy, today I send you my best wishes for the first time from a foreign country. Nevertheless my good wishes for your birthday are as sincere as always. Perhaps if you are not yet here for my birthday you will definitely be here the month after. Therefore don't cry, we shall soon see each other again. Look forward to you birthday happily and think that 39 years ago you were born in London and this year you will return. To your place of birth one can take the tram for one penny. Many congratulations

Herbert

My dear family,

I received your letter last night. You do not have to bring things with you, though the gas cooker would be useful. Next to our room is a small area that can be used as a kitchen. The luggage has still not arrived.

Love and kisses – Herbert

Herbert's parents arrived safely in England in August 1939 but then Herbert was evacuated to Yaxley. Here is one of the postcards he received from his father soon after he arrived at The Vicarage. It is post-marked 8th September 1939.

Dear Herbert,

This morning we received your postcard and hope that meanwhile you have received the package that we sent you yesterday. I hope you no longer feel so home-sick. I heard that school will start soon.

Lots of kisses from Daddy.

The following card was written to his family from the Isle of Man internment camp and shows how well Herbert had progressed with his English in the year since he arrived.

Port Erin
9.7.1940

My dear all!

Because Mama wrote yesterday a letter to you, she can not write this week. We have received the nice parcel and thank you so much. Mama was very glad about all the things and will write next week. Please tell to everyone also to aunt Gisa our thanks. Please send with the other things a brush for cleaning suits in our room in the cupboard and Knopflochgummi.* It is in Mamas Neadlework–basket. Mama has a nice birthday today. Now we was in the cinema.

Kisses Herbert

The following final inclusion from the Levy family letters is written two years later and is an official Red Cross letter from Herbert's aunt, living in England, to her mother, Herbert's grandmother, still in Berlin. These were cruelly official forms leaving little room for communication and the reply had to be written on the reverse side of the letter and not to consist of more than 25 words.

Red Cross letter
16.7.1942

Communication of 4th March received. Hope, and would be reassured if you could get into an old-age home. Desperately awaiting your further news. We are all well. Love to all, Charlotte.

reply on reverse

Am well except for my leg. Will depart tomorrow with Aunt Hannah. Will remain there. Will not come back here. Do not worry. Love to all,

Mother.

Herbert Levy wrote, "Last letter received from my grandmother before deportation to Theresienstadt, and Auschwitz."

*Button–holed elastic

HAROLD NICOLSON
1886-1968

Sir Harold Nicolson married the writer Vita Sackville-West in 1913. The marriage was one of the strangest and happiest and is candidly recorded in *Portrait of a Marriage* by their younger son Nigel. In 1930 the Nicolsons bought Sissinghurst Castle where they lived for the rest of their lives. They restored the house and Vita created one of England's most famous gardens. There were two sons, Ben (Benedict), born in 1914, and Nigel, born in 1917. Both of them served in the army in the Second World War and were sent overseas, Ben to Cairo and Khartoum in October 1942, and Nigel to Algiers a few weeks later. Every Sunday until June 1945 Harold Nicolson wrote, without fail, from Sissinghurst, first to Ben and then a joint letter. The original went to Ben, the carbon copy to Nigel. The first letter was written immediately after Ben's departure. In an extract from his diary we read:

"Ben and I walk round to the Temple Underground, carrying his big fibre suit-case and his funny little handbag. We have to wait some time for the train, but eventually it lumbers through the tunnel. We sit beside each other for the short journey between the Temple and Charing Cross. I cannot speak. When the train stops, I get up and go. 'Goodbye, Benzie.' 'Goodbye, Daddy.' I close the carriage doors behind me. I stand there waiting for the train to go out. It jerks away, taking Ben to Paddington and then to Bristol and then to Avonmouth and then to Lagos and then to Cairo. My eyes are blinded with tears."

Sissinghurst
25 October 1942

I have no news, since I saw you three hours and forty-four minutes ago. It was really horrible shuffling out on to the platform and hearing the train-door grate as it closed. It was *l'adieu supreme des mouchoirs*, and I feel as if I had been knocked down by a bus. But none of us really has cause for self-pity. We have had love and understanding and interesting work in which we have all done well. Nothing can take that from us, and although my heart aches at this moment, yet I know that there is no need for unhappiness, which always comes from frustration or false relationships or muddled personal affections.

This problem of displacement has never been really well expressed. It seems unaccountable to me that I should still be using the same cardboard box of cigarettes which I used at the Club last night and which I bought when you bought a fountain-pen. The box will go to salvage in a few hours, and the pen will go to hazards whence no tears can win it. It seems unaccountable to me that the present should so suddenly (at 8.13 am. on a Sunday) become the past, that the familiarity of King's Bench Walk should be succeeded by the unfamiliarity of a cabin, and that the voices you know should be merged with the voices that you do not know. It is a theme that never ceases to perplex me.

Bless you, my darling Ben, and may God preserve you from suffering or fear . . . .

THE DICTATOR'S DAUGHTER

1935–1938

JOSEPH STALIN SVETLANA ALLILUYEVA
1879–1953 b.1926

Born, according to his internal passport, "Josif Djugashvili, peasant from the Gori District of Tiflis", Joseph Stalin rose to become the supreme ruler of the Soviet Empire for almost 30 years. As a boy he sang in the church choir, was noticed and encouraged and entered a seminary. There his rebellion took root, he joined a socialist study group and was expelled. At 20 years of age he had chosen his faith, Marxism, and his future, revolutionary. Stalin was first exiled to Siberia in 1902, but he escaped and became a prominent Bolshevik revolutionary, noted as a man of action. In 1917 he returned from yet another spell in Siberia to join the Revolutionary Government. From then until 1924 he manoeuvred, as a master of bureaucracy, first to become General Secretary to the Party, and finally to succeed Lenin. Once established as Soviet Leader Stalin imposed policies of indescribable hardship on sections of the Russian people, in which millions died of starvation or execution. He also ruthlessly removed all real or imaginary opponents in a series of purges; on one day, the 12th December 1938, he authorised the execution of 3167 prisoners. Nevertheless, his public image was of the genial father of his people and their great leader during the war. Only after his denunciation by Nikita Khrushchev in 1956 did the full horrors of his reign begin to emerge.

His daughter, Svetlana Alliluyeva, was brought up in Zubalovo with her parents and later her grandfather. It was a happy childhood at first. It was only later, when the family moved to the Kremlin, that she watched it disintegrate. However, these letters between Svetlana and her father are written from a happier time.

Alliluyeva's relationship with her mother was unemotional. There was no lack of love but high expectations and an aloof strict approach were adopted by this beautiful woman. Her father, on the other hand, was quite different. He was physical and warm, always gathering her in his arms and smothering her with kisses. Here is the man who was responsible for the death of millions behaving in a soft sentimental way over the upbringing of his little daughter.

She was aged between four and five years when the following two letters were written. They are printed in block capitals and Stalin's nicknames for her are "Setanka" and "Housekeeper". Apparently he called her this because he wanted her to take an active part in running the household. Alliluyeva said, "Whenever I asked him for anything he liked to answer, 'Why are you only asking? Give an order, and I'll see to it right away.' That's how we started the game of 'orders', which we played until I was about sixteen." He signed all his letters in exactly the same way: 'From Setanka-Housekeeper's wretched Secretary, the poor peasant J. Stalin.' She answered in the same vein, sending him 'orders' which she left for him about the house. He apparently loved this game and almost obsessively never had enough of it, demanding more and more 'orders' from his beloved daughter. However, Alliluyeva grew a little tired of it all and in February 26th 1937 she sent him this appeal: "I order you to permit me to send you an order only once a week."

When she was very little (about three or four) Stalin thought up another game. He invented a perfect little girl named Lelka as an example for Svetlana to follow. Lelka always did exactly what she was supposed to do!

To my housekeeper, Setanka.

You don't write to your little papa. I think you've forgotten him. How is your health? You're not sick, are you? What are you up to? Have you seen Lelka? How are your dolls? I thought I'd be getting an order from you soon, but no. Too bad. You're hurting your little papa's feelings. Never mind. I kiss you. I am waiting to hear from you.

Little Papa

Hello, Setanka!

Thank you for your presents. Thank you for your order, too. I see you haven't forgotten Papa after all. When Vasya and his tutor go off to Moscow, stay and with for me in Sochi. All right? I kiss you.

Your papa

In the summer Stalin would often write to Alliluyeva from Sochi whilst she stayed at Mukholatka in the Crimea with her nurse.

Hello, My Little Sparrow!
Don't be angry with me for not answering right away. I was very busy. I'm alive and well. I feel fine.
I give my little sparrow a big hug.

My Dear Setanka!
I got your letter of September 25th. Thank you for not forgetting your little papa. I'm all right. I'm well, but I miss you. Did you get the peaches and pomegranates? I'll send you some more if you order me to. Tell Vasya to write me, too. Goodbye, then. I give you a big kiss. Your little papa.

She was then aged eight years. The next year, in a letter dated October 8th 1935 he was still sending her fruit!

8 October 1935

Little Housekeeper!
I got your letter and postcard. I'm glad you haven't forgotten your little papa. I'm sending you a few red apples. In a few days I'll send tangerines. Eat them and enjoy yourself. I'm not sending Vasya any because he's doing badly in school. The weather is nice here. Only, I'm lonely because my little Housekeeper isn't with me. All the best, then, my little Housekeeper. I give you a big kiss.

The exchange of presents continues for the next few years.

7 July 1938

Hello, my little sparrow!
I got your letter. Thank you for the fish. Only, I beg you, little Housekeeper, don't send me any more fish. If you like it in the Crimea, you can stay at Mukholatka all summer. I give you a big kiss. Your little papa.

My dear little secretary, I hasten to inform You that Your Housekeeper got an "excellent" in her composition! Thus, she passed the first test and has another tomorrow. Eat drink to your heart's content. I send my little papa a thousand kisses. Greetings to the secretaries.

Housekeeper

This was written on the eve of the Second World War when Svetlana was aged 15, and Svetlana Alliluyeva says that thereafter no one was in the mood for games and jokes any more. However, her nickname stuck and they always remembered with great fondness the game of 'orders'. From then on Stalin became a more remote figure who had little time or interest in his children or grandchildren. Nevertheless, at the time of his terrible and painful death in 1953, Svetlana Alliluyeva sat by him and nursed him and by her account, was flooded with thoughts of grief and love.

"I thought what a bad daughter I was, that I'd been more like a stranger than a daughter to him and had never been a help to this lonely spirit, this sick old man when he was left all alone on his Olympus. Yet he was, after all, my father, a father who had done his best to love me and to whom I owed good things as well as bad – more good than bad, in fact."

THE THIRD REICH

1939–1945

UNITY MITFORD
1914–1948

Unity was one of seven children. Her parents were David Freeman-Mitford, second Lord Redesdale, and Sydney, his wife. Unity's sister, Diana, married the Fascist leader, Sir Oswald Mosley in Berlin with Dr Josef Goebbels providing the house for the wedding reception. This introduced Unity to Germany and she was to become friends with Hitler and thereafter an ardent supporter. He even found her a flat in Munich. However, war was inevitable and on Sunday 3rd September the British consulate telephoned to tell her there was a telegram for her. She went round and was given the news that Britain was about to declare war. She sat straight down and wrote this letter to her parents:

Darling Muv and Farve,

I came round to the Consulate to get your telegram and hear that war has been declared. So this is to say good-bye. The Consul will kindly take this to England and send it to you. I send my best love to you all and particularly to my Boud when you write. Perhaps when this war is over, everyone will be friends again, and there will be the friendship between Germany and England which we have so hoped for.

I hope you will see the Fuhrer often when it is over.
With very best love and blessings,
Bobo.

Fondest love to Blor.

And I *do* hope Tom will be all right.

Unity then went to see Adolf Wagner, Gauleiter of Munich, at the Bavarian Interior Ministry. She knew him well and the office was open, despite it being a Sunday, because of the international crisis. She gave him a large envelope and said goodbye. The envelope contained a Nazi party badge, a signed photograph of Hitler with a personal dedication, and a letter to Hitler. She then walked round to the Englisher Garten. In her handbag was a little automatic pistol that she had bought in Belgium. As soon as she was alone she put the pistol to her right temple and fired.

Unity Mitford survived as a brain-damaged invalid until 1948.

DIETRICH BONHOEFFER
1906-1945

Dietrich Bonhoeffer was one of eight children. He was to become a distinguished theologian whose strong opposition to Nazism cost him his life. He was born in Breslau and studied religion in Berlin and New York. In 1931 he became a Lutheran pastor. In 1939 he fled to America to avoid serving under a Nazi regime but he returned a month later because he felt that in order to be a true Christian he had to take a strong stand against Hitler. In 1943 he was arrested by the Gestapo in the house of his parents and eventually, when they had found proof that he had joined a plot to kill Hitler, taken to Buchenwald. He was hanged by the Nazis in 1945. His parents Karl and Paula provided a loving and stable family background and showed great reserves of courage and faith during the year and a half that Dietrich was in prison. These letters were writen during that time. 'Maria' is Maria von Wedemeyer, his fiancee.

Charlottenburg,
10 June 1943

My dear boy,

. . . . Another parcel is going off to you tomorrow; we fill it with all our love. Each one thinks about what he can contribute, even the little ones. So today there are the few sweets. They all ask after you so much: when are you coming back? We're so grateful that you're healthy. After Whitsun we're going to try again to see you at the Judge Advocate's, as we did last time. Perhaps it well be possible. We aren't really vexed in any way, but it will be allowed. I wanted to send you Reuter's *Ut mine Stromtid*, but couldn't find it, so I'm now sending the *Festungstid* . . . .

I long to hug you.
Your Mother

Tegel
17 December 1943

Dear parents,

There's probably nothing for it but to write you a Christmas letter now to meet all eventualities. Although it passes my comprehension why they may possibly still keep me here over Christmas, I've learnt in the past eight and a half months that the unexpected often happens, and that what can't be changed must be accepted with a *sacrificium intellectus*, although the *sacrificium* is not quite complete, and the *intellectus* silently goes its own way.

Above all, you mustn't think that I'm going to let myself be depressed by this lonely Christmas; it will always take its special place among the other unusual Christmases that I've kept in Spain, America, and England, and I want in later years to look back on the time here, not with shame, but with a certain pride. That's the only thing that no one can take from me.

Of course, you, Maria and the family and friends, can't help thinking of my being in prison over Christmas, and it's bound to cast a shadow over the few happy hours that are left to you in these times. The only thing I can do to help is to believe and know that your thoughts about it will be the same as mine, and that we shall be at one in our attitude towards the keeping of this Christmas. Indeed, it can't be otherwise, for that attitude is simply a spiritual inheritance from you. I needn't tell you how I long to be released and to see you all again. But for years you have given us such perfectly lovely Christmases that our grateful recollection of them is strong enough to put a darker one into the background. It's not till such times as these that we realize what it means to possess a past and a spiritual inheritance independent of changes of time and circumstance. The consciousness of being borne up by a spiritual tradition that goes back for centuries gives one a feeling of confidence and security in the face of all passing strains and stresses. I believe that anyone who is aware of such reserves of strength needn't be ashamed of more tender feelings evoked by the memory of a rich and noble past, for in my opinion they belong to the better and nobler part of mankind. They will not overwhelm those who hold fast to values that no one can take from them.

From the Christian point of view there is no special problem about Christmas in a prison cell. For many people in this building it will probably be a more sincere and genuine occasion than in places where nothing but the name is kept. That misery, suffering, poverty, loneliness, helplessness, and guilt mean something quite different in the eyes of God from what they mean in the judgment of man, that God will approach where men turn away, that Christ was born in a stable because there was no room for him in the inn – these are things that a prisoner can understand better than other people; for him they really are glad tidings, and that faith gives him a part in the communion of saints, a Christian fellowship breaking the bounds of time and space and reducing the months of confinement here to insignificance.

On Christmas Eve I shall be thinking of you all very much, and I want you to believe that I too shall have a few really happy hours, and that I am certainly not allowing my troubles to get the better of me. It will be hardest for Maria. It would be marvellous to know that she was with you. But it will be better for her if she's at home. It's only when one thinks of the terrible times that so many people in Berlin have been through lately that one realizes how much we have to be thankful for. No doubt it will be a very quiet Christmas everywhere, and the children will remember it for a long time to come. But it may perhaps bring home to some people for the first time what Christmas really is. Much love to the family, the children and all our friends. God bless us all. With much gratefulness and love.

Your Dietrich

Prinz–Albrecht–Strasse
28 December 1944

Dear mother,

I'm so glad to have just got permission to write you a birthday letter. I have to write in some haste, as the post is just going. All I really want to do is to help to cheer you a little in these days that you must be finding so bleak. Dear mother, I want you to know that I am constantly thinking of you and father every day, and that I thank God for all that you are to me and the whole family. I know you've always lived for us and haven't lived a life of your own. That is why you're the only one with whom I can share all that I'm going through. It's a very great comfort to me that Maria is with you. Thank you for all the love that has come to me in my cell from you during the past year, and has made every day easier for me. I think these hard years have brought us closer together than we ever were before. My wish for you and father and Maria and for us all is that the New Year may bring us at least an occasional glimmer of light, and that we may once more have the joy of being together. May God keep you both well.

With most loving wishes, dear, dear mother, for a happy birthday.

Your grateful Dietrich

Charlottenburg,
28 February 1945

Dear Dietrich,

We've heard nothing of you since your departure from Berlin, and I expect that you've heard nothing from us. Nothing has happened to us during the many recent raids apart from the breakage of a couple of panes of glass. So you needn't worry. All the rest of the family are still in good health. Maria is at present taking her sister, who has fled from the East, to relations, so mother is doing my appointments as well as the house. It's a lot for her on top of all the other things that a large family involves. We're worried about your health. We would like to send your washing and the other things that we could otherwise send, but so far we haven't found any way of doing it. I hope that Christel will bring some news from the Prinz-Albrecht-Strasse today. If it's possible, do send us some message soon. Old people like ourselves ought to have permission to write more frequently. Affectionately,

Your Father

My dear Dietrich,

My thoughts are with you day and night. I'm worried how things may be going with you. I hope that you can do some work and some reading, and don't get too depressed. God help you and us through this difficult time.

Your old Mother

We are staying in Berlin, come what may.

KLAUS BONHOEFFER
1901–1945

Klaus Bonhoeffer was an older brother to Dietrich Bonhoeffer. Klaus studied law at Heidelberg and, after obtaining his doctorate and spending a year in England studying international law, he worked in Geneva for the League of Nations. In 1930 he married Emmi Delbrueck and they had three children, Thomas, Cornelie and Walter. He saw the dangers of National Socialism long before 1933 and predicted war as soon as Hitler became Chancellor. He and many members of his family became involved in the resistance movement against Hitler and he was arrested by the Gestapo in October 1944 in the aftermath of the plot to kill Hitler on 20th July 1944. He was condemned to death and shot on 22nd April 1945 along with his brother-in-law. Unknown to him, his brother, Dietrich and another brother-in-law had been executed earlier that month. His parents learnt of his and his brother's death via the broadcast by the BBC of a memorial service held for them in the Holy Trinity Church, Kingsway, London.

This is his last letter to his children written from prison.

Easter 1945

My dear children!

I won't live very much longer and so I want to say goodbye to you. I find that very difficult; because I love each of you so very much and you were nothing but a joy to me. Now I shan't see how you grow up and become independent. But I am quite confident that as you take Mama's hand you are going to proceed on the right road and that you will find advice and help in our relatives and friends. Dear children, I have seen much and experienced even more though my fatherly experiences will not be able to guide you. Therefore I want to tell you a few things which are important for your life even though you might only understand some of it later. Most of all, stay close to Mama, in love, trust, gallantry and caring as long as God keeps her with you. Always think about whether you can't give her some joy. I hope that once you are grown up you might be as close to your mother as I always was to my parents because you only really understand you parents when you are grown up yourself. I asked Mama to stay with me until the end. These were difficult but magnificent months. They were directed towards the essential and were carried by your mother's love and strong spirit. You will understand that only later.

Keep close and ever closer as brothers and sisters, too. It is because you are so different from each other that you sometimes find reason to quarrel. But once you are older you will be able to give each the more for it. The occasional quarrel isn't so bad but don't harbour it. Think of me, then and give each other your hands happily (i.e. make peace easily). Help each other wherever you can. If one of you is sad or in a bad mood look after him until he's cheerful again. Don't just leave each other, look after him and that will bring you together again. Play, sing, dance with each other the way we used to. Don't go off on your own with your friends when your brothers and sisters could take part. That also strengthens a friendship.

I wear the ring on my right hand with which Mama has made me happy. It is a symbol that I belong to her and also to you. The Crest ring on my left hand reminds me of the family we belong to – those before and after ourselves. It says, "Listen to the voice of the past. Don't lose yourself arbitrarily in the present. Stay faithful to the good ways of your family and pass them on to your children and grandchildren." Dear children, do understand properly this particular duty. Respect for the past and responsibility for the future give you the right attitude for life . . . .

LITERARY DAUGHTERS

1950–1963

SYLVIA PLATH
1932–1963

Sylvia Plath was born in Boston, Massachusetts in 1932. After attending Smith College she won a Fulbright scholarship to Cambridge University where she met the English poet Ted Hughes. They were married in 1959. For a short time they taught in America and then she and Ted returned to England where they settled in Devon and had two children, Freida and Nicholas. Her collection of poetry, *The Colossus* appeared in 1960. She had a history of depression and had attempted to take her own life more than once before coming to Cambridge. Her experiences whilst receiving treatment, particularly the electric shock therapy, is reflected in her only novel *The Bell Jar* and in her prose piece, *Johnny Panic and the Bible of Dreams* as well as in a number of her poems. She wrote over a thousand letters to her mother (Aurelia Plath) and in them we can detect the fragile nature of her character. Her mood swings are often violent and disturbing. When Sylvia Plath was happy she records it with a vivacity and intensity that is almost terrifying. Her lows are more controlled and contained and the more disturbing because we detect the struggle going on within. Sylvia Plath committed suicide on 11th February 1963 in London, having separated from Ted Hughes. It was one of the coldest winters on record. The following is her first letter written from Smith when she was 18.

Smith College
Northampton, Mass.
27 September 1950

Dearest Mummy,

Well, only five minutes till midnight, so I thought I'd spend them writing my first letter to my favorite person. If my printing's crooked, it's only because I drank too much apple cider tonight.

Even though I don't have much finery adorning my room yet, it seems that it's pretty much home. Tangible things can be awfully friendly at times. Even though I've only been here since three, an awful lot seems to have happened. I kind of like getting a quiet first acquaintance with my room and the girls.

I feel that I've wandered into a New York apartment by mistake – the maple on my desk feels like velvet. I love my room and am going to have a terrific time decorating it.

I lay down for half an hour and listened to the clock. I think I'm going to like it – the ticking is so rhythmic and self–assured that it's like the beat of someone's heart – so–o–o it stays on the bureau.

> For a time Sylvia then seemed to write to her mother every day and appeared to be enjoying life. However, her letters become less frequent when dark moods and homesickness creep into her life. She eloquently communicates this with her mother.

July 7, 1951

Dear Mummy,

. . . . I feel very sorry I don't write more often, Mumsy, because your letters are great sustenance to me. I miss you and home and Warren, and wouldn't mind so much if I felt I was *learning* anything, or writing or drawing something worthwhile – When there is no one around to make you feel wanted and appreciated, it's sort of easy to talk yourself into feeling worthless. I haven't really *thought* about anything since I've been here. My reactions have been primarily blind and emotional – fear, insecurity, uncertainty, and anger at *myself* for making myself so stupid and miserable.

. . . . *Seventeen* sent two brief mimeographed copies of eulogistic letters about my story. I laugh a bit sadistically and take them out to read whenever I think I'm a worthless, ungifted lummox – some gal by the name of Sylvia Plath sure has something – but who is she anyhow?

"My head is bloody, but unbowed,"

May children's bones bedeck my shroud.

X X Sivvy

P.S. I *will* grow up in jerks, it seems, so don't feel my growing pains too vicariously, dear. Love you all heaps.

After several years of study, intermingled with editing for the magazine *Mademoiselle*, writing and suffering from depression and the consequent treatment of electric shock therapy, Sylvia came to England. The "ex–Cambridge poet" referred to in the following letter was Ted Hughes.

Cambridge
Saturday Morning
3 March 1956

Dearest Mother

. . . . Had sherry at Chris Levenson's Thursday with Stephen Spender and others. When I get a few more recent (and more sociological) poems ready, I'll send them to his magazine. One thing, British Literary circles are so *inbred*; every writer ends up in London, knowing everything about the work, mistresses and personal idiosyncrasies of everyone else, and talks and analyzes the others continually. Blessed be America for its catholic *bigness!*

Met, by the way, a brilliant ex–Cambridge poet at the wild *St. Botolph's Review* party last week; will probably never see him again (he works for J. Arthur Rank in London), but wrote my best poem about him afterwards – the only man I've met yet here who'd be strong enough to be equal with – such is life. Will send a few poems in my next letter so you can see what I'm doing.

Much, much love,
Sivvy

Sylvia continues to write ecstatic letters over the next year until her marriage in July 1956. Her first baby, Frieda was born on April 1, 1960, in London: " I looked on my stomach and saw Frieda Rebecca, white as flour with the cream that covers new babies, little funny dark squiggles of hair plastered over her head, with big, dark-blue eyes . . . ."

The next year Sylvia, Ted and Frieda moved to Devon. She continued to write and enjoyed being in the country, cooking and homemaking while Ted became increasingly famous. Their son Nicholas Farrar was born on January 17, 1962, but by June of that year their marriage was in serious trouble. She continued to write frequent, lengthy letters to her mother and in July Aurelia visited the family in Devon, but she sensed the tension. That was the last time she was to see Sylvia. By October of that year Sylvia's letters contain definite cries for help. In December she closed the large house in Devon and, leaving Ted, moved with the children to a flat in Yeats' former home in London. The winter of 1963 was terrible, with thick snow and very low temperatures. Sylvia had flu. She tries to reassure her mother but life becomes an increasing struggle.

Wednesday, January 16,1963

Dear mother,

Thanks very much for your letter and the cheque. I am slowly pulling out of the flu, but the weakness and tiredness following it makes me cross. I had a day nurse for a week when I was worst and the children had high fevers (little Frieda got a ghastly rash, which turned out to be an allergy to penicillin, which she can't have), but then the nurse got a cold and went home, just as well, for she used up that $50 cheque; they are very expensive. The children are themselves again, thank goodness . . . .

The weather has been filthy, with all the heaped snow freezing so the roads are narrow ruts, and I have been very gloomy with the long wait for the phone, which I *hope* to get by the end of the month after two month's wait, which makes me feel cut off, along with the lack of an "au pair".

. . . . I just haven't felt to have any *identity* under the steamroller of decisions and responsibilities of this last half year, with the babies a constant demand. Once I have an "au pair," the flat finished – after all, it is furnishing for at least five years and should always be my "london furniture," so it is an investment – and a phone and routine, I should be better, I think.

. . . . But I get strength from hearing about other people having similar problems and hope I can earn enough by writing to pay about half the expenses. It is the *starting* from scratch that is so hard – this first year. And then if, I keep thinking, if only I could have some windfall, like doing a really successful novel, and *buy* this house, this ghastly vision of rent bleeding away year after year would vanish, and I could almost be self-supporting with rent from the other two flats – that is my dream. How I would *like* to be self-supporting on my writing! But I need *time*.

I guess I just need somebody to cheer me up by saying I've done all right so far. . . .

One month later, on February 11th 1963, Sylvia Plath was found dead. She had killed herself by putting her head in the gas oven. She was only thirty years old and at the height of her powers.

SAPPHO DURRELL
1951–1985

Sappho Durrell was the second daughter of the novelist Lawrence Durrell. She was born in 1951 in Oxford, the daughter of the second marriage. (Lawrence Durrell was married four times.) After the birth the family returned to Cyprus, where her mother, Eve Cohen, had a nervous breakdown and asked Lawrence Durrell's mother to move in to look after Sappho. Two years later Eve and Lawrence Durrell separated and Sappho moved to England with her mother. However, she continued to visit her father regularly and developed a close relationship with his new wife, Claude. When Sappho was sixteen Claude died of cancer.

Much of what Lawrence Durrell wrote was based on his life and Sappho believed that she was the inspiration for one of Durrell's characters, Livia, from the novel of the same name. Livia is a changeling, a monster and is said to have been a girl forged from a boy, who dreamed she had sex for the first time with a man who resembled her father and later became lesbian. Livia dies by suicide: she hangs herself.

Sappho wrote copiously, including journals, a play about Emily Bronte and dream notebooks, and corresponded frequently with her father. In 1979 Sappho underwent psychoanalysis. During this period she wrote extensively about her complex feelings towards her father. "I feel, when I'm with him – or writing to him – that I am on his black side. We quarrel over a shirt label; he will not give in over a single detail of reality. I am frightened of him physically and mentally."

On 31 January 1985 Sappho Durrell committed suicide. Five years later Lawrence Durrell died.

The following letter from Sappho to her father is in response to a letter she has received from him in which he has urged her to approach her psychoanalysis sessions seriously. He has signed the letter 'Lover'.

14 June 1979

Dearest Pa

Many thanks for the lovely letter. The only bit I didn't like was the unkind reference to my 'rat-like super-ego'. I shall cross swords with you for that you old fart! As for psychoanalysis: you may be right but I'm playing it entirely by ear. At the moment everything has stabilized out and I feel a lot lighter.

We seem to be in for some traditional spring weather her for a change now that the Conservatives are back with their Good Goddess rain-bearing Maggie. Pudding Island has signed its death pledge and it's toy-town all the way to the grave, I fear. Maybe not.

I'm having fun welding my Bronte sketches together. Branwell is something of a tough nut because he comes across so much (in researches) as a joke figure. But then there are two versions of him (of course) and in EJB's mind something else rather interesting is going on . . . .

Proof-reading a book called *Animals are my Best Friends* (the truth guv!) ghost-written for the Director of the Dublin Zoo in such sub Gerry (yes, it *is* possible)-stroke-Irish whimsy that the Director himself felt moved to scoop some off with a trowel – insisting on drastic readjustments so that he could hold his head up in the Dublin bars. Oh these small delights. Almost as touching as A. L. Rowse's subconscious – but not quite.

I shall know when I feel better: when I feel able to face Bernard Stone and all that awful millpond again. There's a good Geiger-counter.

Give us a ring to let us know how things are going *chez toi*. Will so ditto. When do you get back from Greece? I wouldn't mind coming down for a stay in Sommieres circa mid-September (which is when I'm free of this literary agent work).

LOTSA LOVE, AS ALWAYS

Saph

In Lawrence Durrell's next letter to Sappho he says that her current troubles have less to do with Freudian neurosis than with the fact that she has been 'trying to grow a prick in the wrong place'. He says it is not only a female problem and mentions an operation he has had himself to remove 'two large lumps of camel fat off my back.'

His letter is re–typed by Sappho and covered with annotations.

16th July 1980

Dear Pa

It was good to hear you yesterday and reassuring to know that you are well. (You've become such a crusty old badger with me that it's hard for me, what with nervousness and the sort of semaphore we speak over the phone, to assess how you are.) So.

Please put aside *at least one* evening between the 18th Sept and 2nd Oct to come and have a slap–up, boozy supper *chez nous*.

The garden is looking very fine so it would be good if it was at a weekend and we could have a kebab lunch outside for starters, Retsina and all – or whatever.

If Anthea's pals' flat falls through, *par hasard*, you are more than welcome to stay here if you can stand to 'rough it' (and I *mean* rough – wait till you see us: we have just knocked down a major wall and are knee-high in plaster dust, and the place is a bit like a Bedouin encampment). But we'd be delighted to have you stay and, as soon as we're straightened out more here, that's an invitation which will have more allure for you than at present.

I hope that Athens was, as the Americans say, a 'gas' (details of the prize got lost in telephone crackle. Which work was it for?).

Lots of love and looking forward to seeing you again soon,

Saph

(PS I wish you would bury your six hatchets once and for all and sound a *little* bit pleased to hear from me when I phone. Do I have to spell out how much it all upsets me?) Lotsa love – S

> The next letter from Sappho to her father is in response to one from her father dated 12 October 1980 in which he expresses relief that she has finally recovered from a nervous breakdown. In his letter he describes his dream of an ideal woman. He is living on his own and missing being looked after.

Dear Pa

At last a moment to sit down and write you a fulsome thankyou for your lovely warm letter. I am relieved that everything physical is ticking over nicely. Your asthma can be eased away with yoga (she says blithely). Certainly you looked in the pink of reassuring health when you were in London. Most probably (models after 1945 having built-in obsolescence) you are in better health than I am. I've given up nurturing the hectic flush on my left cheek.

(It was also heartening to get a warm response last Sunday. Here's hoping that this last week was fruitful and some good work has come of it.)

Simon and I are in the last stages of disembowelling the downstairs rooms to make one L-shaped living-room and have plaster dust all over again. Us and the cats coughing and sneezing our way around and dredging bits of lath out of our tea (not the cats . . . .). I am soon rid of two of the three cats. This will rank as Bliss in the First Degree. One self-important cat is absolutely adequate for me. (Simon is also relieved.)

O where are you going to find this good woman? Is none of your beautiful American correspondents going to prevent you wasting away? (What an awful paradox in the land of plenty.) Incidentally, attended an *absolutely magical* concert of eleventh–thirteenth century music: troubadour songs and poems; Bernart de Ventadorn, Jaufre Rudel de Blaye, Marcabru, Guillaume de Marchaut, Gace Brule, Guilhem IX, Guirat Riquier, Mermot d'Arras. With luck I may be able to make a recording of it as it is being broadcast her in November. The sounds ranged from those akin to delicate Indian Ragas to Irish peasant ballads (no surprise in this, but it was a delightful, spirited perfor-mance throughout, as well). Funny, memorable, haunting. All in Provencal with intermittent translation her and there. Fingers crossed for a recording. Anthea is coming to supper tomorrow, and I'm afraid the place is like a skip. Never mind. One must chuckle.

Lots of love. Keep up the good work, and for goodness sake don't waste away. I hope that Xmas here wouldn't disperse you too much. See how you feel nearer the time. I have my free days booked (a certain amount of crude arm–twisting here) with some difficulty, so you'd better, or else .... by then we shall have a workable spare room if Les Brontes cannot materialise.

In any event, lots of love and look after yourself. Will write again when I have a moment. Good and happy novelling–

Saph

13 July 1981

Dear Pa

Thank you for a delightful refreshing week. I wish it could have been for longer. Back in shabby London where the weather is strangely thundery and hot. I shall get the Schopenhauer pamphlet to you in the course of the next week or so. Incidentally, the novel I mentioned to you is by Salman Rushdie and is called *Midnight's Children*. The Mozart *Cosi Fan Tutte* recording which you will enjoy (if it's still in print) is by Karl Bohm with Elizabeth Schwarzkopf *et al* and is a genuine delight – funny, sad, triumphant. Keep me posted on news and let me know in advance of any change of plans.

LOTS OF LOVE, of course

Saph

MODERN WARS– VIETNAM AND THE FALKLANDS

1962–1982

VIETNAM WAR
1962–1972

The Vietnam war began for the USA in 1962 when the Americans sent military advisors to South Vietnam to help prevent an invasion by the Viet Cong, the communist North Vietnamese. Soon, however, the US were combatants and their involvment rapidly escalated into a massive commitment of men and the most modern of weapons. The war ended in 1972 with the USA withdrawing and Vietnam united under the government of the North. The Vietnam War had the most profound effect on the USA. It was the first war in which, because of television, the people at home saw the stark reality of war and not what the Military and Government wanted them to know. It was also, perhaps, the first war in which a nation's young rebelled and said, "No, we want no part in this."

Dear Dad,

Well here it is. We've been told the whole company will be shipping out to Vietnam after advanced infantry training. Our Company Commander and Battalion and Brigade Commander have told us there's no sense in trying to fool ourselves, we're going for sure. The only thing that makes me mad is how do they expect us to tell our parents. I don't mind going but there are some guys here who just won't make it. And I don't think they'll make it out alive.

Your son

P.S. Tell Mum not to worry. It's nothing I can't handle.

SP/5 RICHARD CANTALL

Hello dear folks

It's going to be hard for me to write this but maybe it will make me feel better. Yesterday my Company was hit while looking for V.C. They told me they needed someone to identify a boy they had just brought in – bad, they said. So I went into the tent. And there on the table was the boy. His face was all cut up with blood all over it. His mouth was open, his eyes were both open. He was a mess. I couldn't really identify him so I went outside while they went through his stuff. They found his ID card and dog-tags. I went in and they told me his name. "Rankin"* – I cried, "No, God, it can't be!" But sure enough after looking at his bloody face again I could see it was him. It really hit me hard because he was one of the nicest guys around. He was one of my good friends. No other K.I.A. or W.I.A. hit me like that. I knew most of them but this was the first body I ever saw and being my friend it was too much.

After I left the place I sat down and cried. I couldn't stop it. I didn't think I ever cried so much in my whole life. I still see his face now. I'll never forget it. Today the heavens cried for him. It started raining at noon and has now finally just stopped after 10 hours of the hardest rain I've ever seen.

love Richard

P.F.C.GEORGE WILLIAMS

Dear Ma,

Vietnam has my feelings on a see-saw. This country is so beautiful. When the sun is shining on the mountain, farmers in the rice paddies with their water buffalo, palm trees, monkeys, birds and even the strange insects – for a fleeting moment I'm not in a war zone at all – just on vacation but still missing you and the family. There are a few kids who hang around, some with no parents. I feel so sorry for them. I do things to make them laugh and they call me "dinki dow". That means crazy. I hope that's one reason we're here – to secure a future for them

Your son George

*P.F.C. Donald Rankin

THE FALKLANDS WAR

LT. DAVID TINKER
1957–1982

David Tinker was born in 1957 in Barnet. Throughout his childhood at school at Mill Hill and later at Dartmouth Naval College and Birmingham University, David was a keen correspondent, writer of poetry and admirer of the war poets.

As a lieutenant in the navy he served on HMS Glamorgan, one of the ships sent to the Falklands after the Argentinians invaded in April 1982. He was to be killed two days before the end of the conflict. His letters from this period are initially of boyish enthusiasm for a jaunt to the South Atlantic, optimistically and naively hoping that the conflict would not escalate. They describe everyday life on board HMS Glamorgan. But as the reality of armed conflict became apparent, David Tinker's naivety matured to cynicism and mistrust of the British Government's actions.

TO HIS FATHER

HMS Glamorgan
22 May 1982 (received, 10 June)

Your long marvellous letter of 6 May arrived today via HMS Leeds Castle (a most inappropriate name for a ship!) which is acting as postman between us and Ascension Island. It was like a breath of sanity coming into this totally mad world here. I am glad that you think that way about Mrs Thatcher and the war – as I have come to think since this business started. I sometimes wonder if I am totally odd in that I utterly oppose all this killing that is going on over a flag. Wilfed Owen wrote that "There'll come a day when men make war on death for lives, not men for flags", but it has been the reverse here – "nations trek from progress" still.

It is quite easy to see how the war has come about; Mrs Thatcher imagined she was Churchill defying Hitler, and the Navy advised a quick war before the winter set in; the Navy chiefs also wanted maximum use made of the Navy for maximum publicity to reverse the Navy cuts: which has happened. For (utmost) worth, victory or defeat would have the same result; publicity and popular support, either congratulations or sympathy. The Navy thus overlooked the fact that we were fighting without all the necessary air cover which is provided by the USA in the Atlantic and by the RAF in the North Sea and Icelandic Sea. Although the Harrier is a marvellous little aircraft it is not a proper strike aircraft, and the best the Navy could get when carriers were "abolished". Consequently, we have no proper carriers which can launch early–warning aircraft fitted with radar as strike aircraft. From the Fifties onwards these two were absolute essentials.

. . . . I haven't mentioned much about the war and our part in it in my letters to Elisabeth and you, and to Christine, so as to try to avoid upsetting and worrying them in addition to the worry they must already feel, especially when the news is so regularly ghastly. However, I will to you, because you know what it's like; with six years' worth, it won't seem so unexpected. We still cannot believe we are at war, even while it's going on, and when I have had a good night's sleep I wake up without remembering the war for a while. Our surroundings, of course, are exactly as normal: and we are very used to doing perpetual exercises. We still have proper food, hot water to wash with, etc. There are a few differences; covers and fabrics have been thrown away, the scuttles (windows) permanently blacked out, the chests tied down, no loose papers about – but life has its flashes of normality. I sometimes have some typing to do, we have "Requestmen" and "Defaulters", the NAAFI sells choco-late, and we still have "Elevenses" (at Stand Easy). As we don't have personal weapons there's no particular feeling that we are fighting. We are mostly a peaceful bunch who would not want to shoot anyone. The war just happens; we do shelling of shore positions and we get attacked by aircraft. We dislike both, and the time when everyone is relaxed and happy is when we are "legging it" away from the action at 29 knots . . . .

I suppose that this sort of naval war is quite different from your war when you had to put up with a lot more – lasting for six years. These last three weeks have seemed long enough and we don't like to think any more into the future that the end of the day. We are lucky in that we can rescue our survivors and send them back to England, and our living conditions are fine; but air attack by these very fast jets coming in low is not very nice.

The pity for us is that there is no cause for this war; and, to be honest, the Argentinians are more patriotic about the Malvinas than we are about the Falklands . . . .

Still, I suppose this is all an experience one should go through if only to drive home for each generation how stupid war is. As Housman wrote:

Ay, yonder lads are yet
The fools that we were them;
For oh, the sons we get
Are still the sons of men.
The sumless tale of sorrow
Is all unrolled in vain:
May comes tomorrow
And Ludlow fair again.

I suppose he would have approved of the irony of a war starting on May 1st: also the anniversary of Gallipoli!

Certainly the trivia of life and the important things are all brought to mind by this. And how much the trivia are at the forefront of normal life and the important things put away, or not done, or left to do later and then forgotten. Here, certainly, the material things are unimportant and human "things", values, and ways of life are thought about by everybody.

David Tinker's last letter from the Atlantic to his parents. It was received on the 30th June, 18 days after he was killed in action.

HMS Glamorgan,
8 June 1982

It seems quite some time since I wrote to you last; I have now received your letters up to 17 May. Thank you very much for them. It is very nice indeed to hear news of the normal world as one has to look very hard in the papers to find anything that is not about war.

. . . . You seem to be very busy . . . . with the proofs of your book, tending to the veggies, and visiting lots of interesting old farmhouses. The descriptions you sent conjured up a lovely picture of Beatrix Potter–type Lakeland scenes (I saw a Beatrix Potter exhibition in Edinburgh – where we called after yet another exercise – in February, where they had the original watercolours of Peter Rabbit . . . . strange, to think that these were the actual drawings from which the prints were taken) . . . .

. . . . Life is very nicely routine here, and everybody is very relaxed and very well. We recently had first crack at a store ship straight out from England, so we are all topped up with food and goodies. We have ice cream for lunch and have even had some apples. The last store ship really used up everything. They even found some butter which had turned green although deep-frozen. It had been laid down as "emergency war stocks" when the ship first commissioned. Incidentally, that was the store ship which sailed to the Gulf with us and was just about to go home from Gibraltar when we were all sent here. She has been away since October 19th, so they will be very glad to get home.

Lots of love for now; I will write again soon.

ACKNOWLEDGEMENTS

The editor and publishers wish to thank the following for giving their permission to use the following material:

Bodley Head for extracts from the letters of Scott Fitzgerald included in *Letters of Scott Fitzgerald* edited by Andrew Turnbull, Bodley Head 1964.

The British Library for reproductions of:

1. Letter of James I to his son Prince Henry. April 1603. Ms.6986 f 65.
2. Letter from Agnes Paston to her son. Ms 34888 f13.
3. Letter from Robert Briffault to his daughter Muriel. October 1917. Ms 58441 ff60/61.

Collins for a letter from Harold Nicolson to Ben Nicholson. *Diaries and Letters 1939-45*, edited by Nigel Nicolson, 1967.

Elspeth Huxley for extracts of Nellie Grant's letters to her and included in *Nellie: Letters from Africa* published by Weidenfeld & Nicholson 1980.

Herbert Levy for the unpublished correspondence between members of his family.

Oxford University Press for a letter to Hans Krebs from his father included in the book, *Reminiscences and Reflections*, published 1981.

Aurelia Plath for letters from Sylvia Plath included in *Letters Home* by Sylvia Plath, edited by Aurelia S Plath. Published by Harper & Row 1975.

Public Record Office who keep the originals of the letter of Mary Basset to Lady Lisle SP.3/1,f87 & James Basset to Lady Lisle. S.P. 3/1, f.66.

The Marquess of Salisbury for the transcript and reproduction of Prince Edward's letter to Henry VIII.

A Biography of G. K. Chesterton by Michael Ffinch, published by Weidenfeld and Nicholson

The editor and publishers acknowledge the following:

Hutchinson & Co for extracts from *Letters to a Friend* translated by Pricilla Johnson-McMillan, published 1967.

Somerset County Archives and Record Office for the letters by William Burridge.

Michael Joseph for extracts from *1914-1918, Voices & Images of the Great War* by Lyn Macdonald, published 1988.

Weidenfeld & Nicholson for extracts of letters of Karen Blixen from *Isak Dinesen, Letters from Africa, 1914-1931*, published 1978.

Harper Collins for extracts from the letters of Ernest Hemingway included in: *Hemingway: Selected Letters, 1917-1961* edited by Carlos Baker, Published Granada,1985.

Granta for inclusion of letters from Sappho Durrell to Lawrence Durrell. Included in *They fuck you up* Granta 37, Autumn 1991.

S.C.M. Press for extracts of letters of Dietrich Bonhoeffer from *Letters and Papers from Prison*, published 1971.

Russel (Michael) Publishing Ltd for extracts of letters from *Letters of Freya Stark* ed. Lucy Moorehead. Published Compton Russel, 1974.

Hugh Tinker for extracts from the letters of David Tinker contained in A *Message from the Falklands, The Life and Gallant Death of David Tinker Lieut. R.n. from his letters and poems* compiled by Hugh Tinker, Published by Junction Books, 1982

The Paston Letters. Edited by Norman Davis. Oxford University Press World Classics.

Letters from Lady Havisia de Neville, Eleanor, Queen Dowager, Edward II, Henry VIII : from *The Voice of The Middle Ages in Personal Letters 1100–1500*, edited by Catherine Moriarty, Lennard Publishing, 1989.

Sir Thomas More to his children: *Latin Epigrams of Thomas More*, edited by Leicester Bradner & C. Arthur Lynch, 1953.

Lisle Letters: Muriel St Claire Byrne, Secker and Warburg, 1983

Madame de Sévigné, Penguin Classics.

Mozart's Letters, translated by Emily Anderson, edited by Eric Blom, Penguin.

The Memoirs of Berlioz, David Cairns, Panther 1970.

The Letters of Gustave Flaubert, translated by Francis Steegmuller, The Belknap Press of Harvard University Press, 1980.

The Letters of Tchaikovsky: *Letters to his Family*, translated by Galina von Meck, Stein and Day, A Scarborough Book, New York.

Letters of Svetlana Alliluyeva: *Letters to a Friend*, Hutchinson, 1967.

Robert Gibson for his translation of two letters of Alain-Fournier contained in his book *The Land Without a Name* published by Elek, 1975.

Anna Freud by Elisabeth Young-Bruehl, published by Macmillan, 1988

Englishmen At War: Social History in Letters 1450-1900 by Ernest Sanger, Allan Sutton Publishers, 1993

Mary Murphy, Archivist, Institute of Civil Engineers

INDEX